DISTANZ

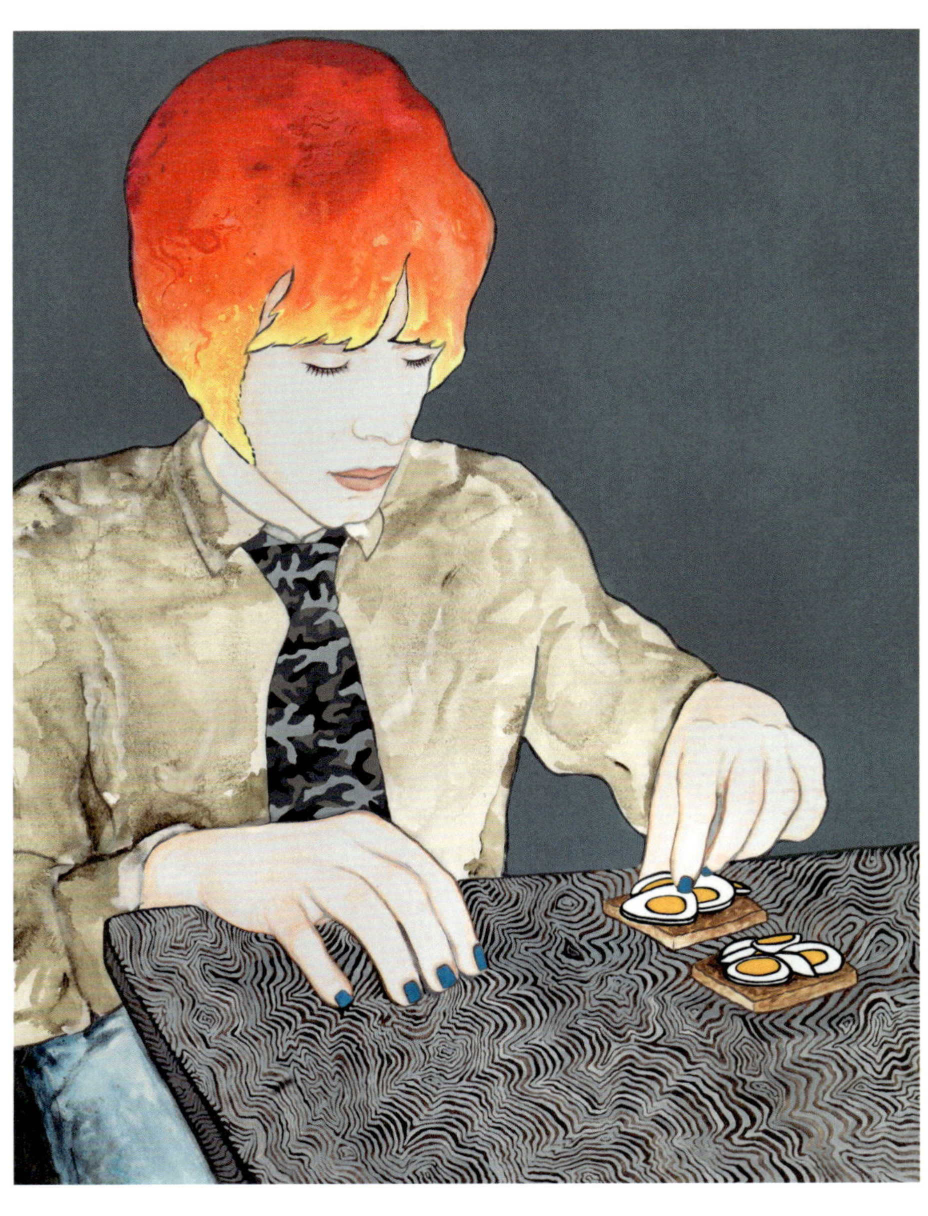

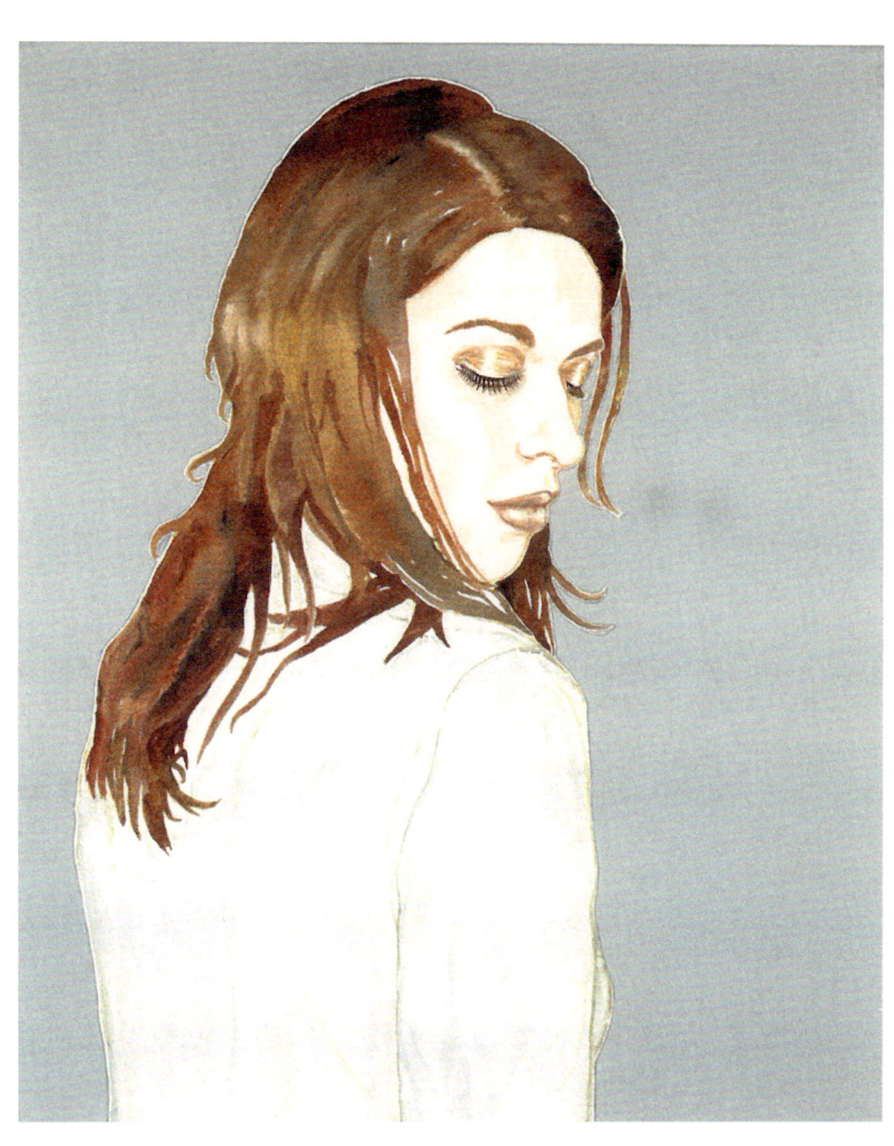

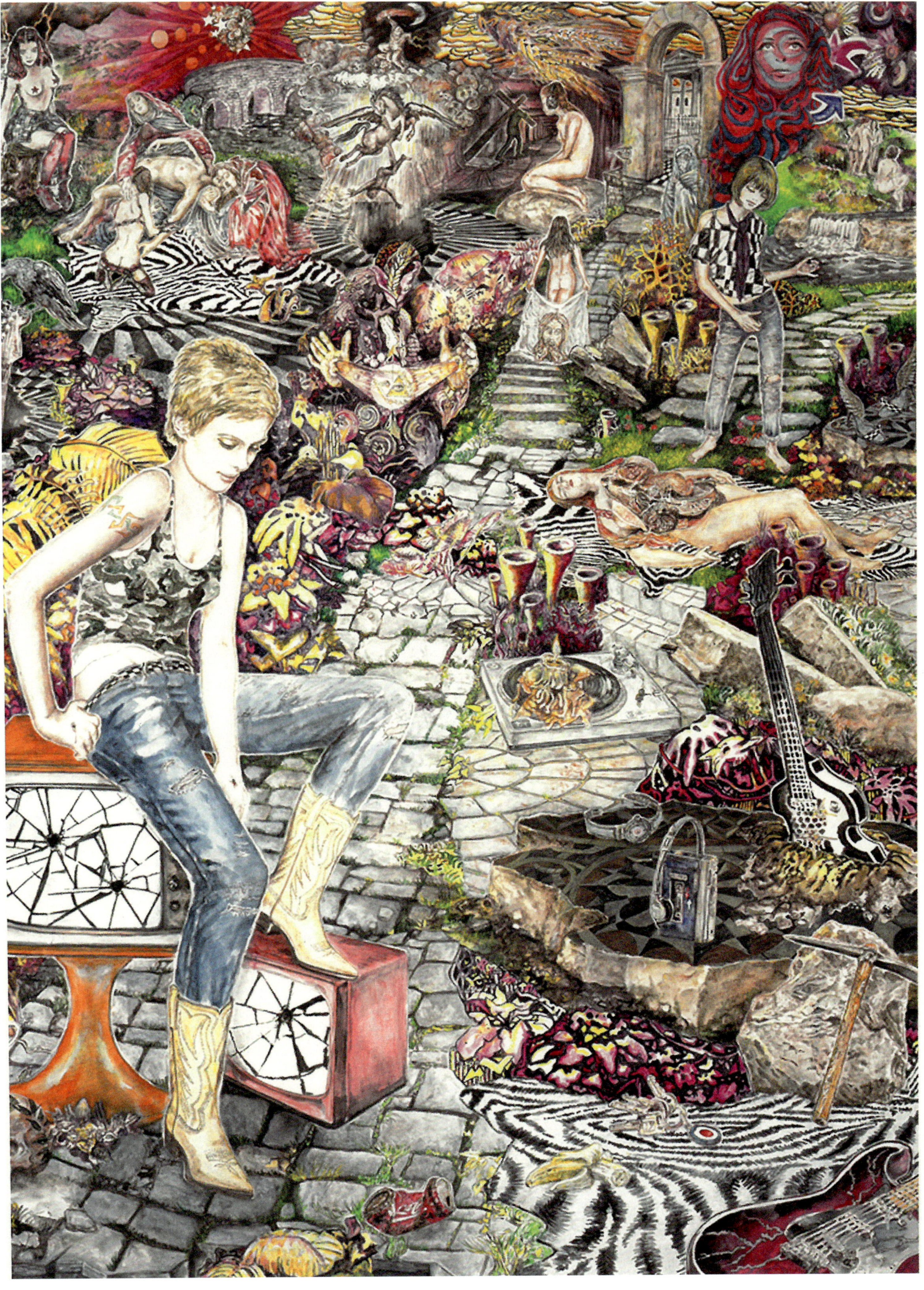

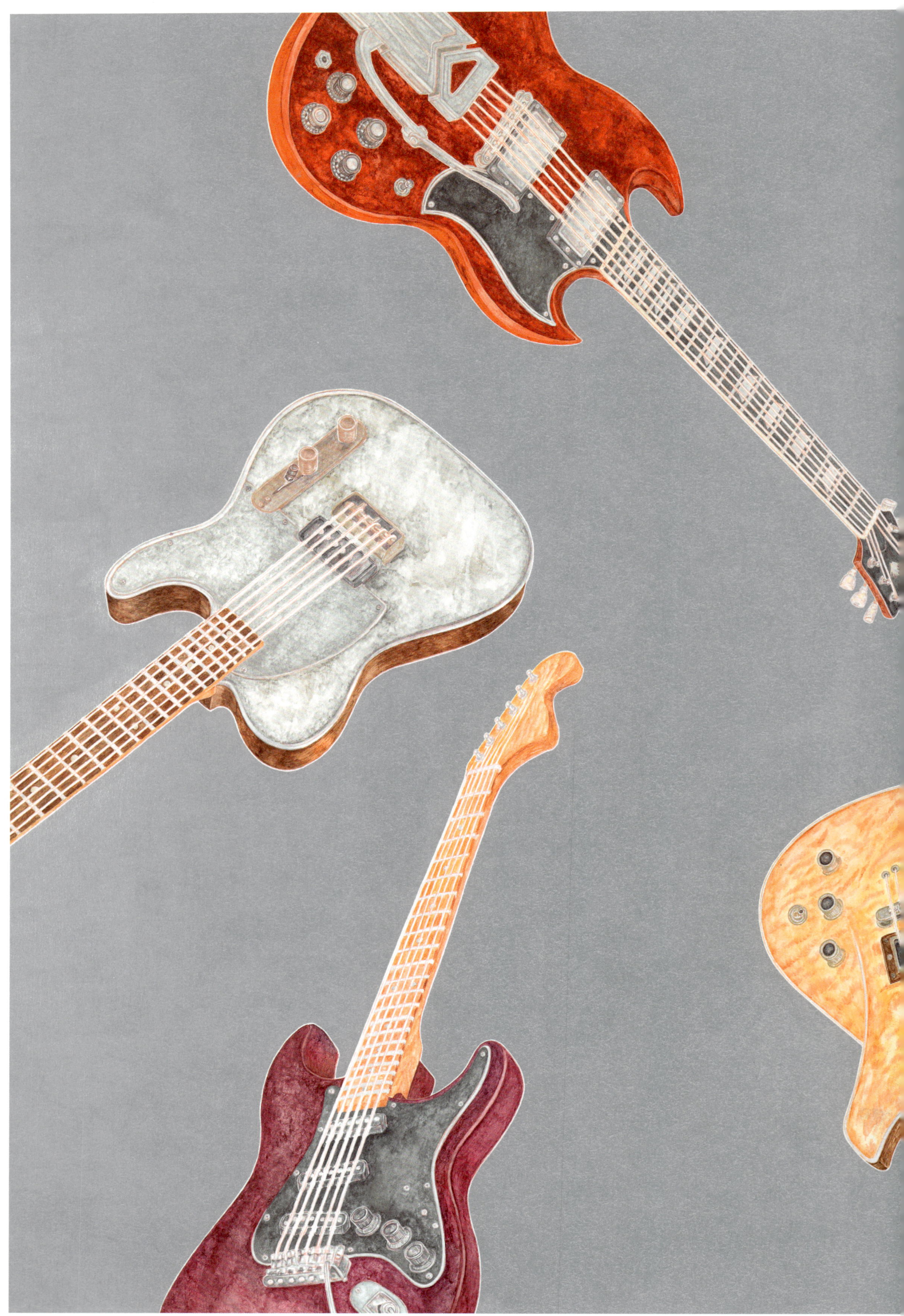

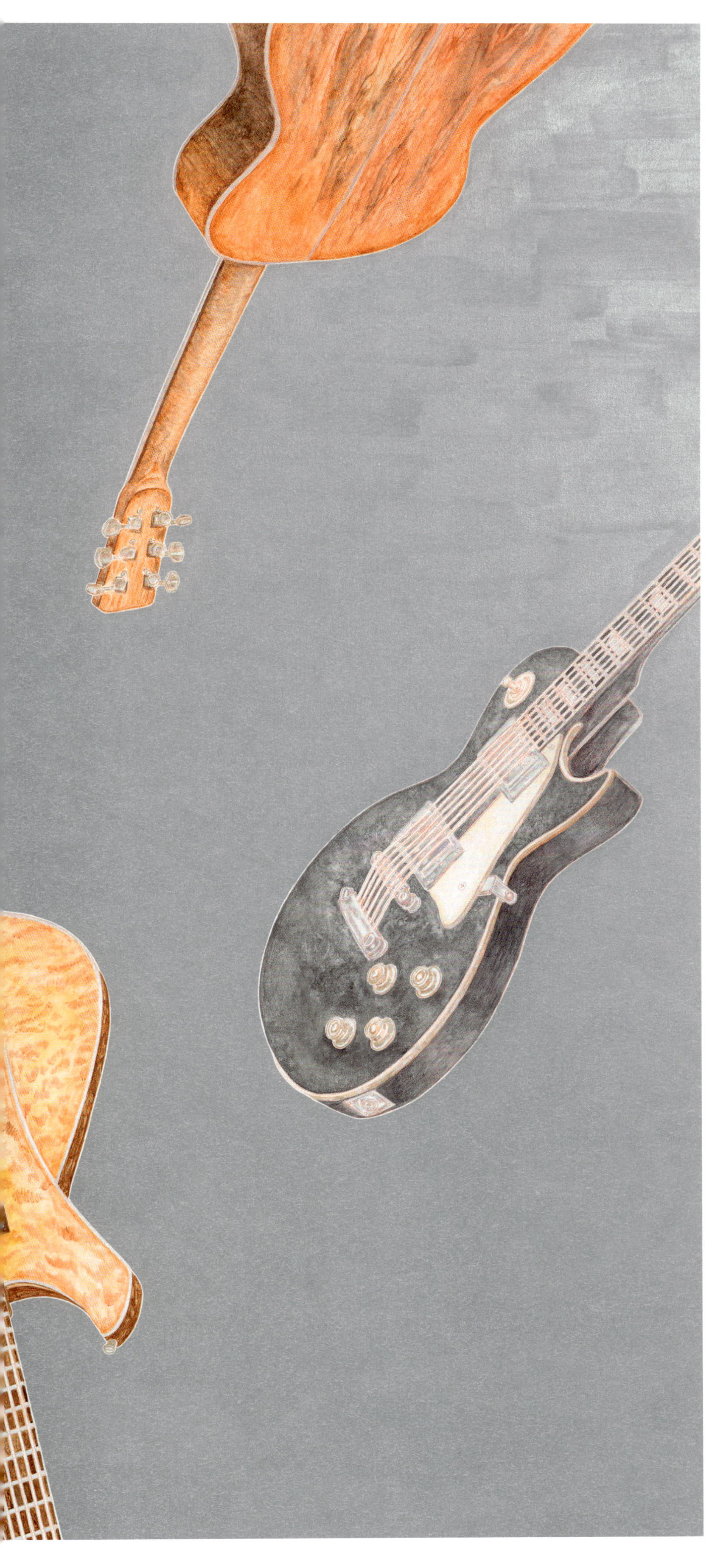

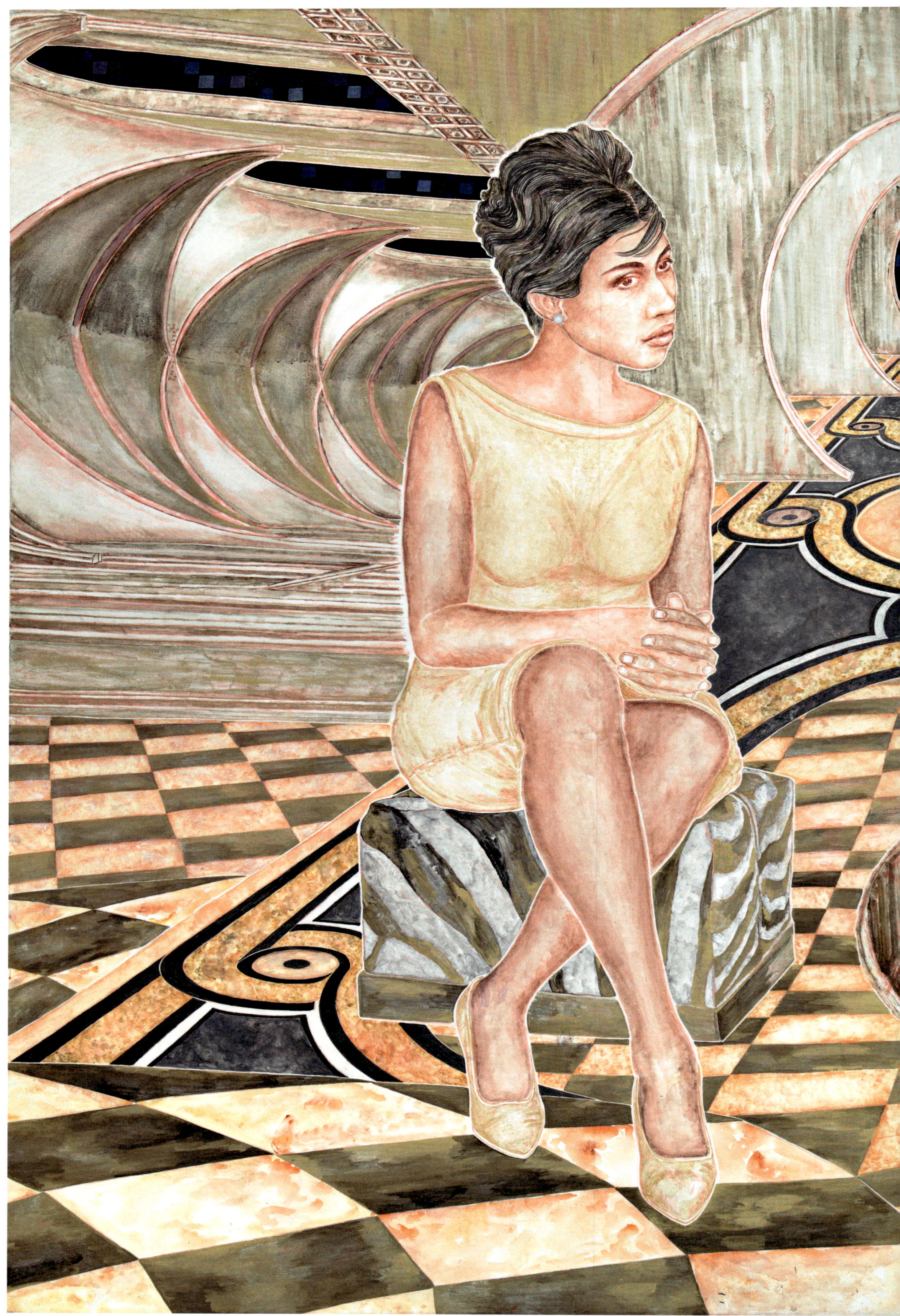

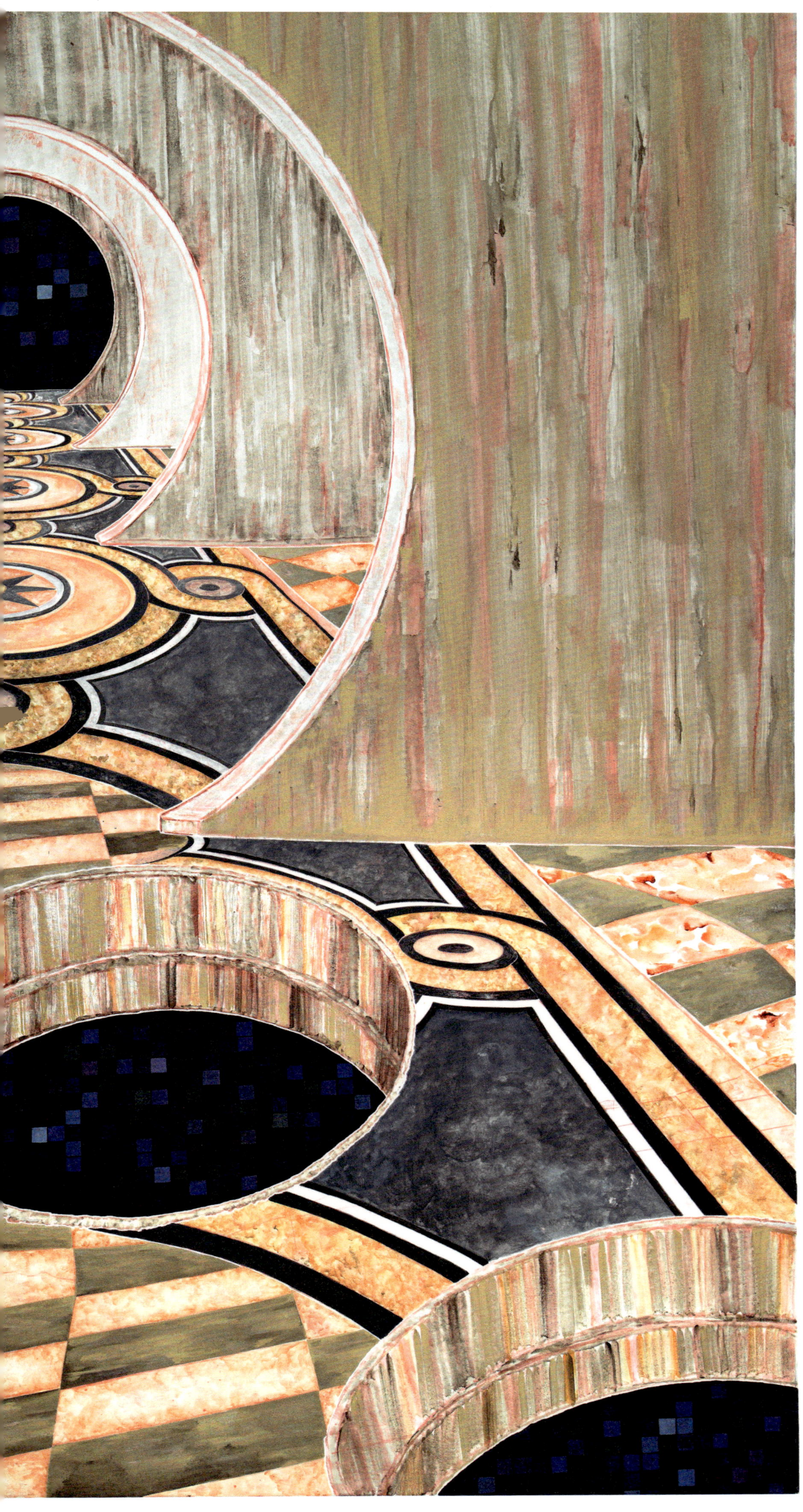

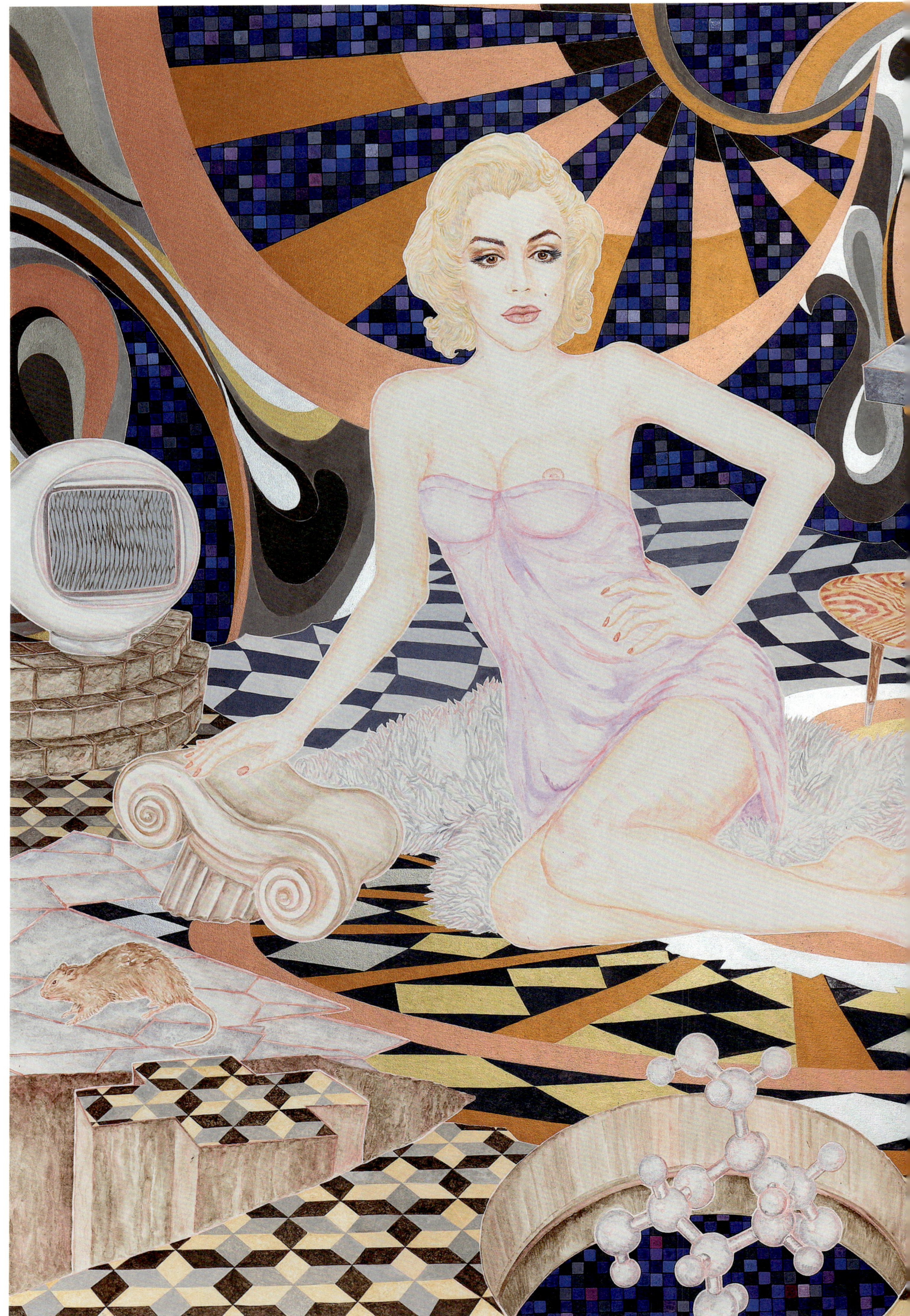

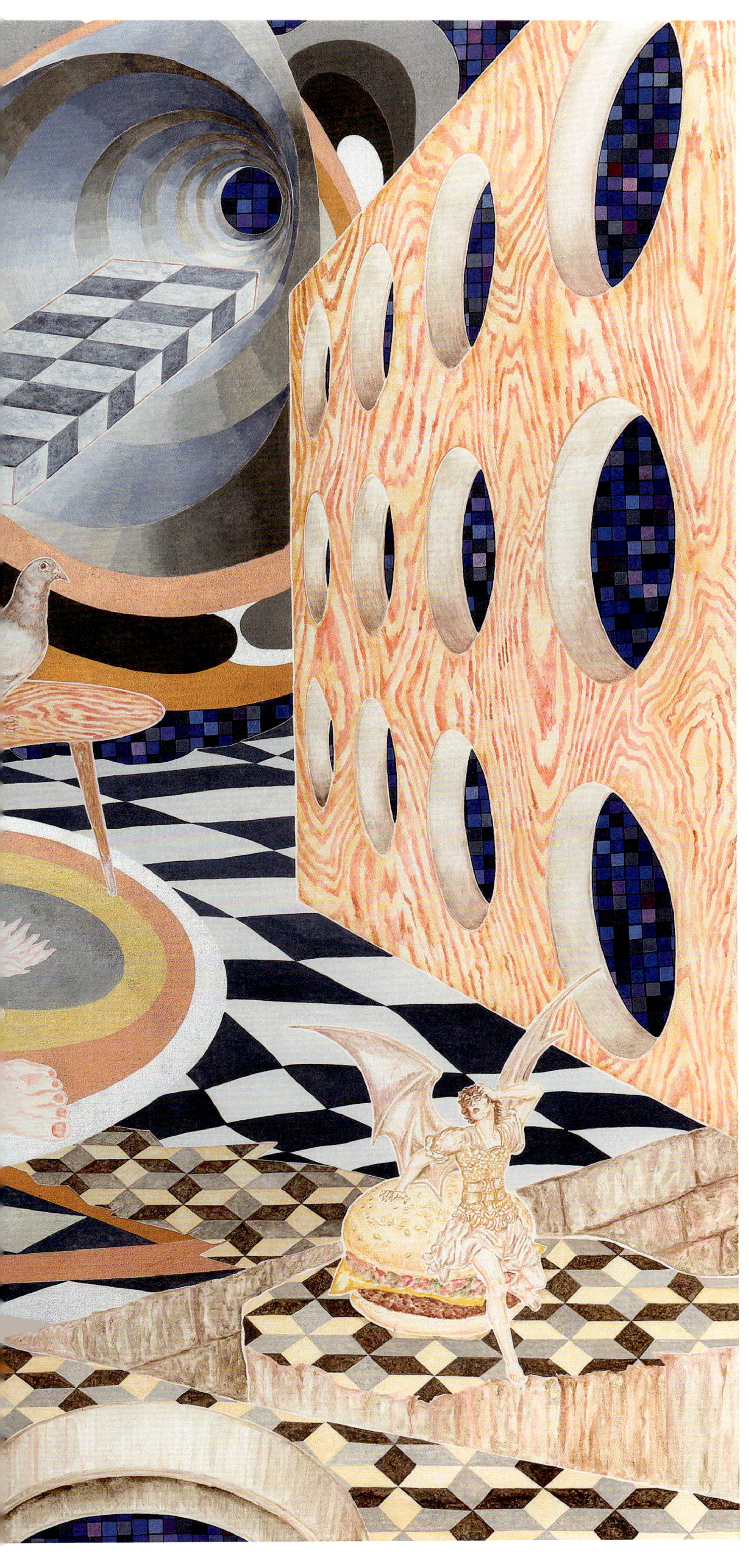

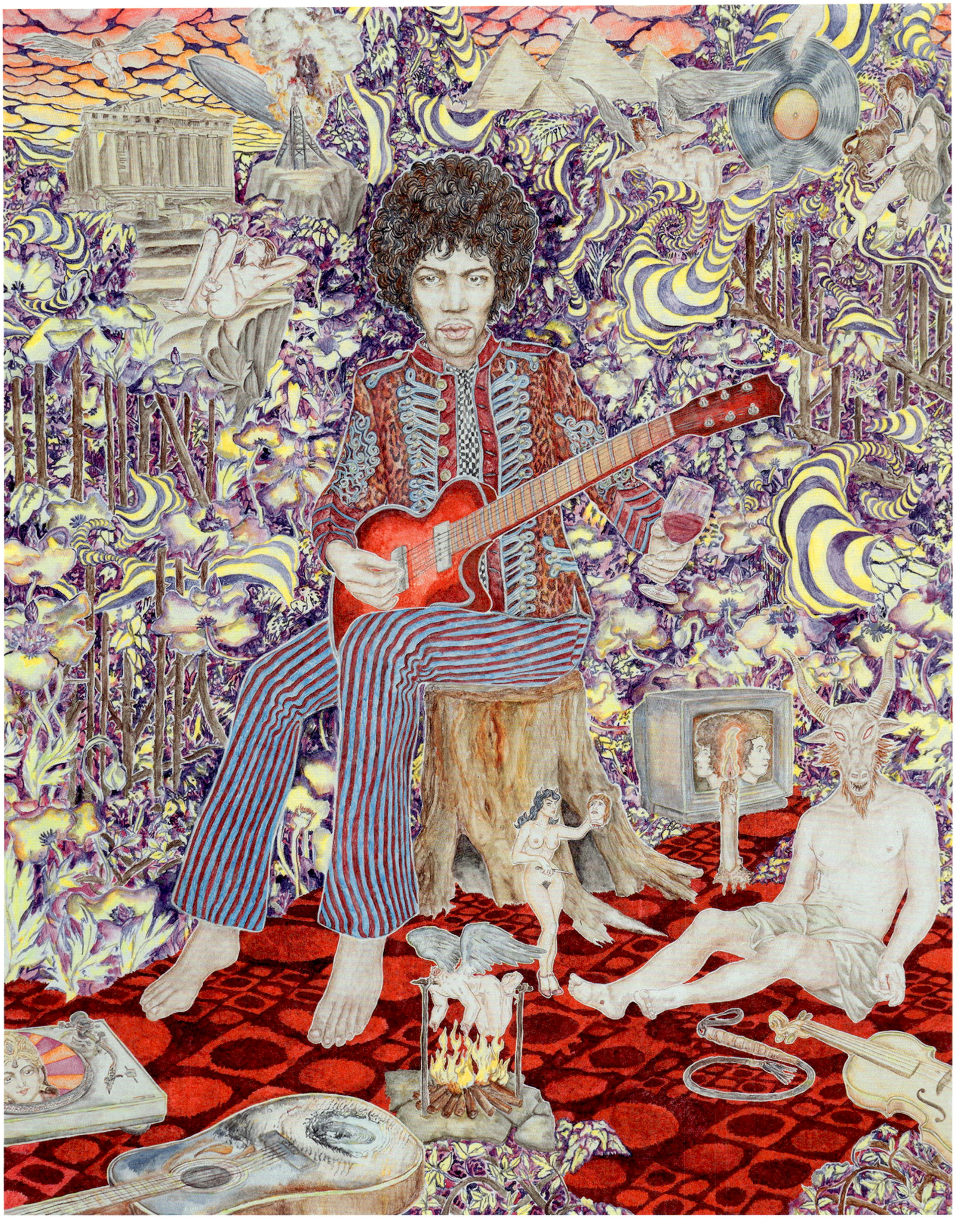

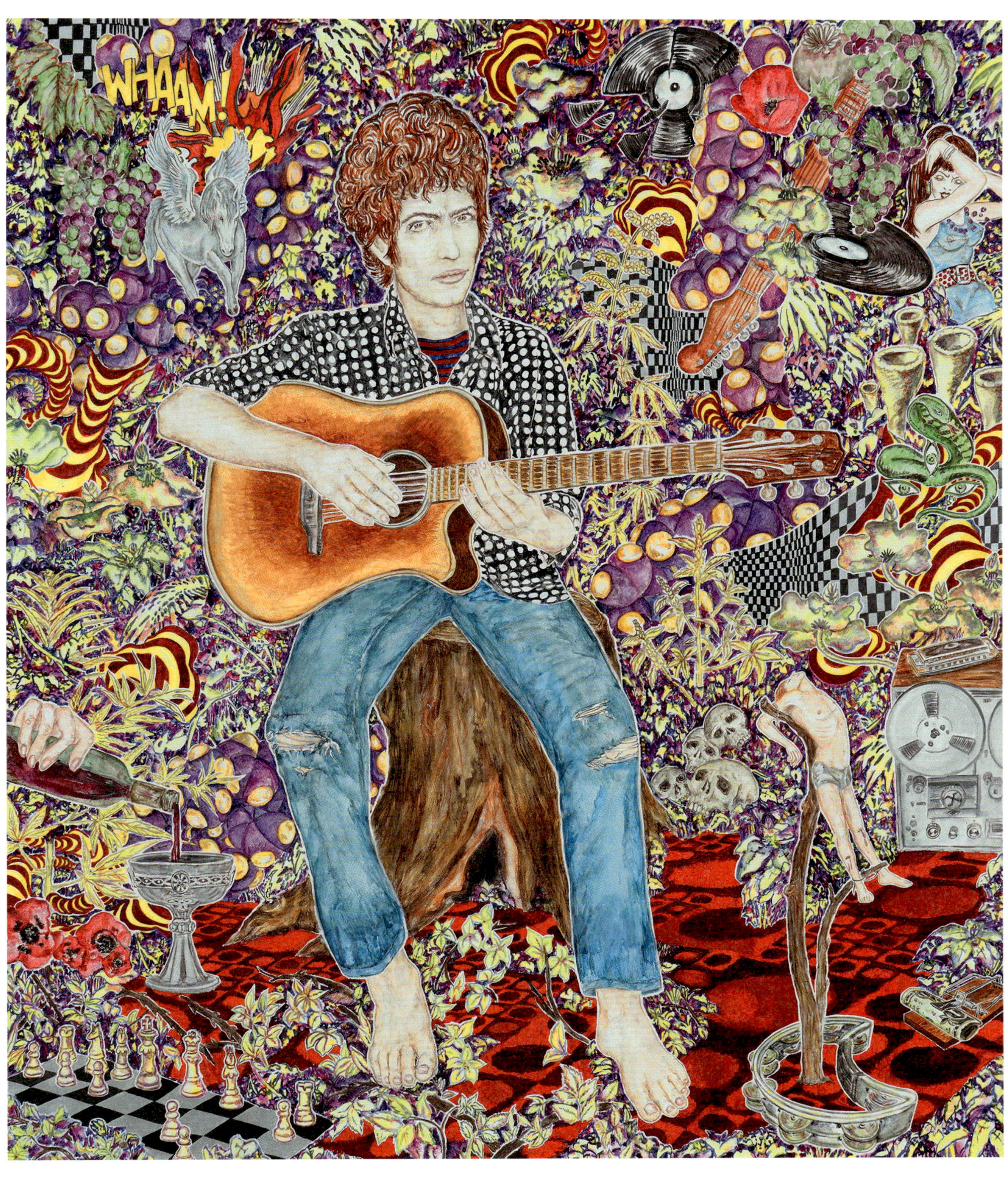
WHAAM!

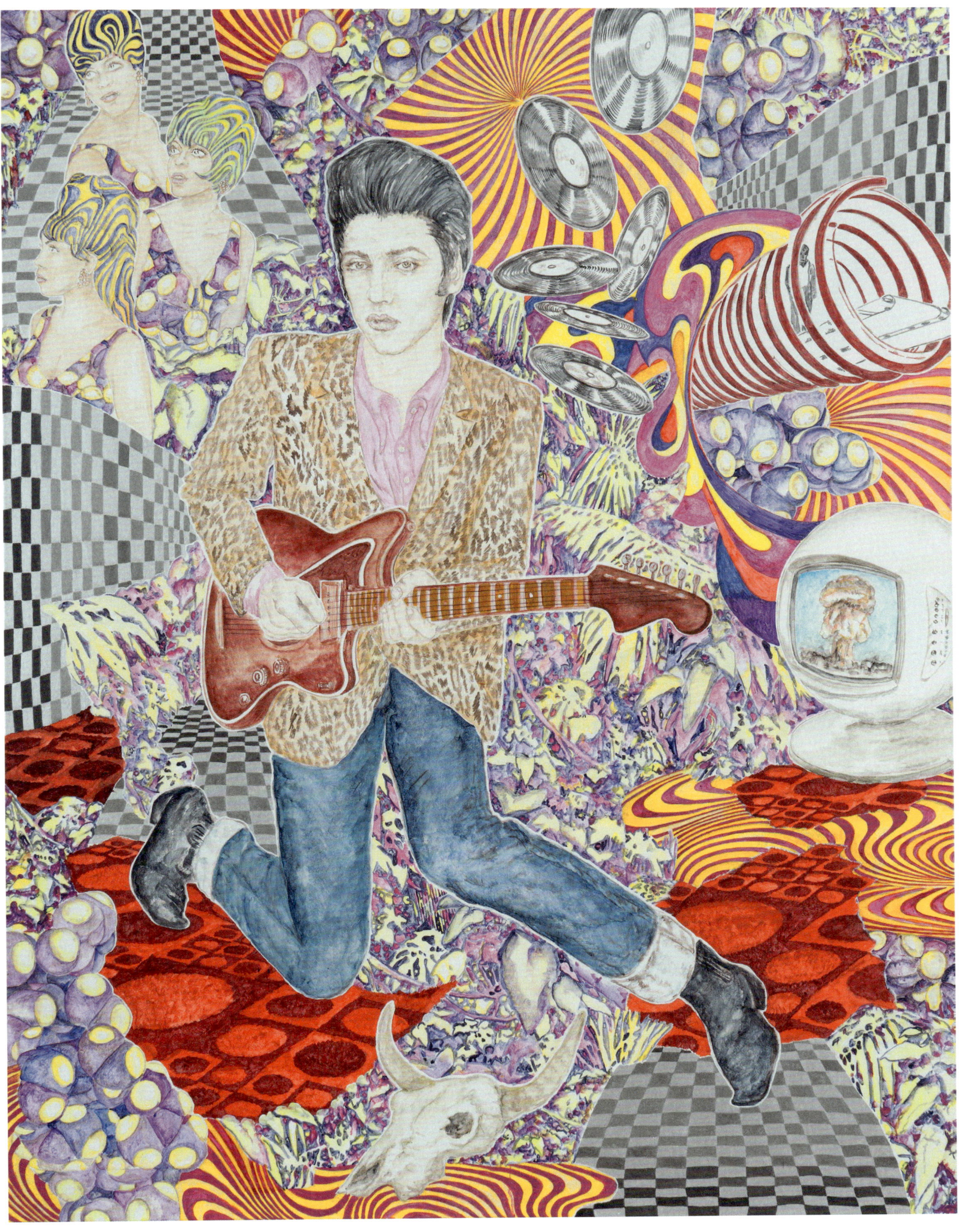

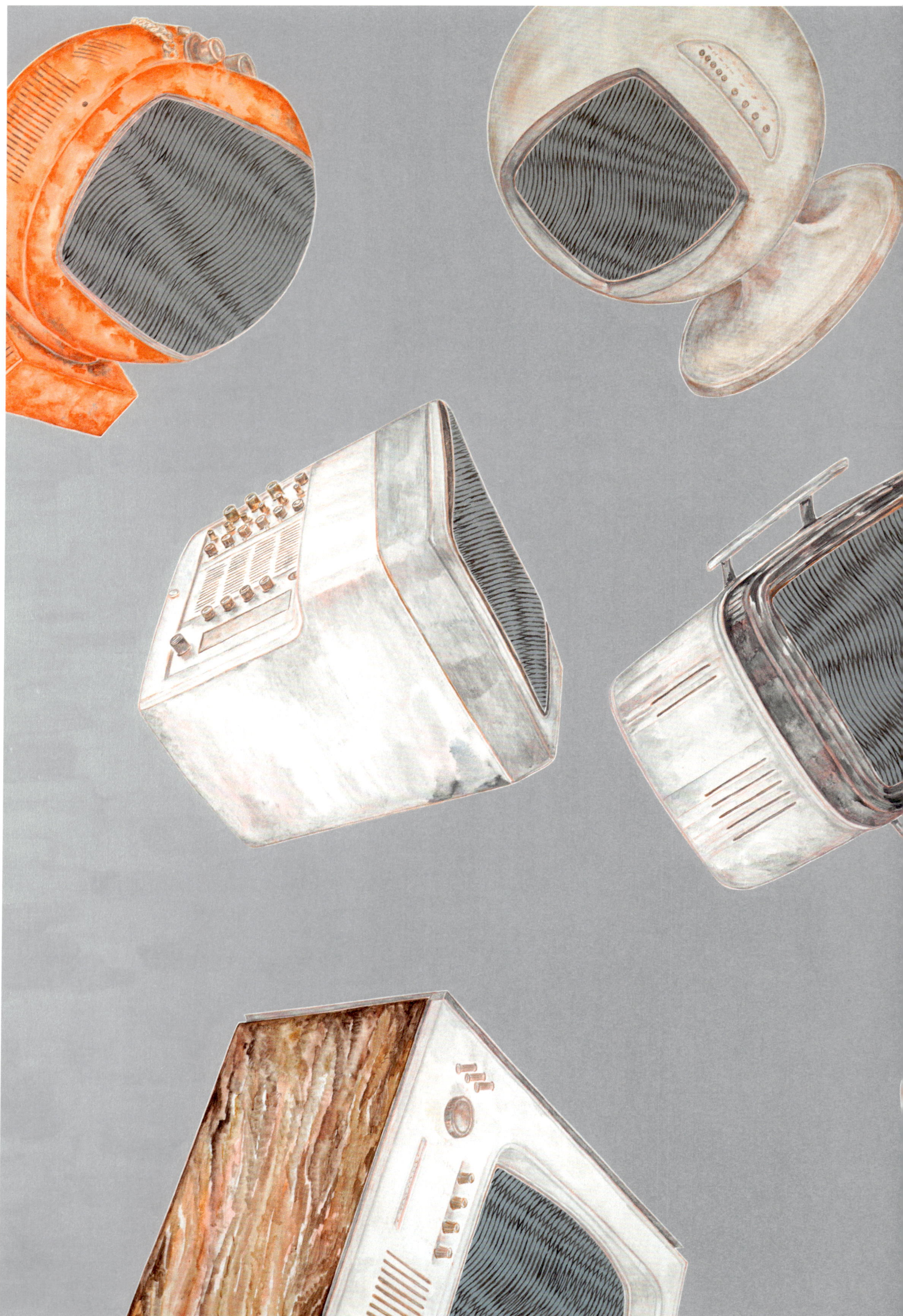

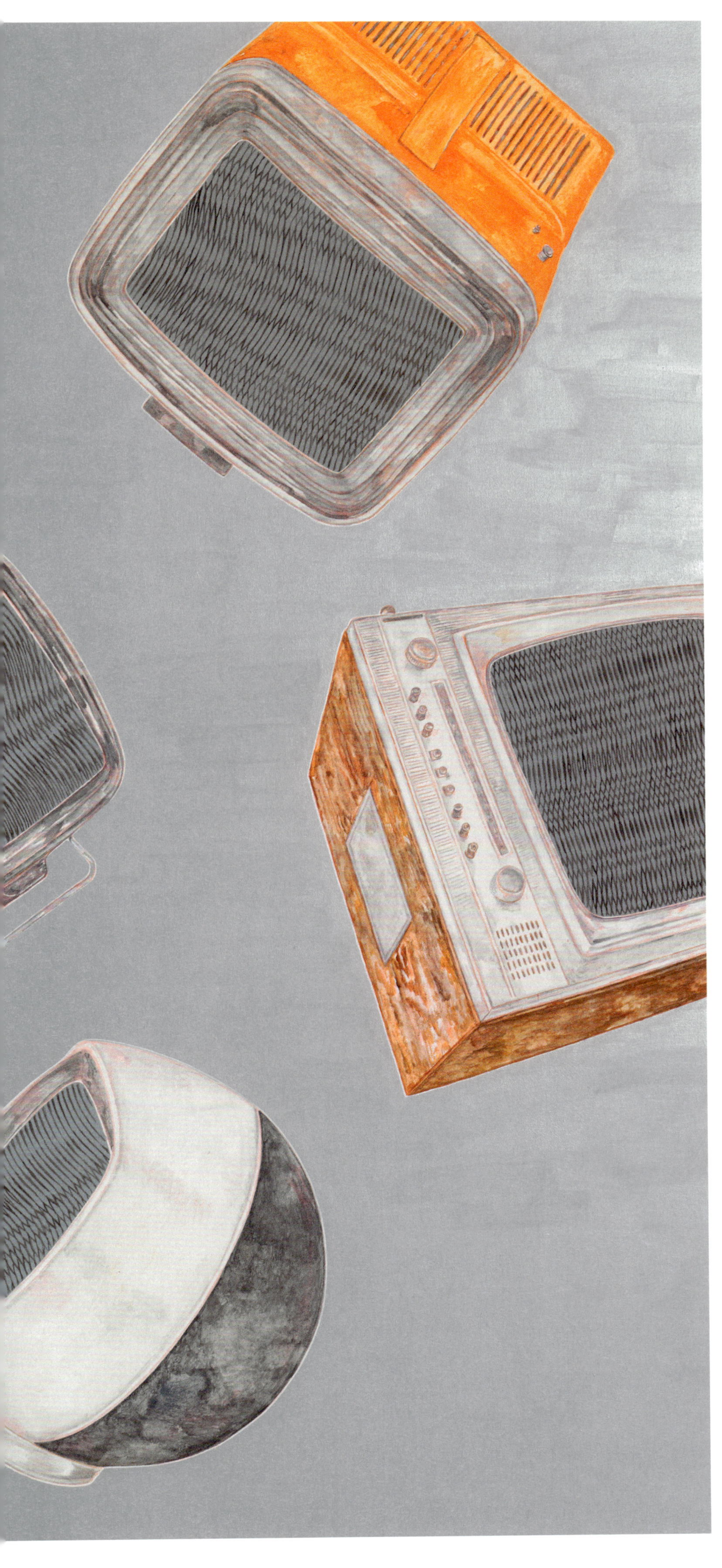

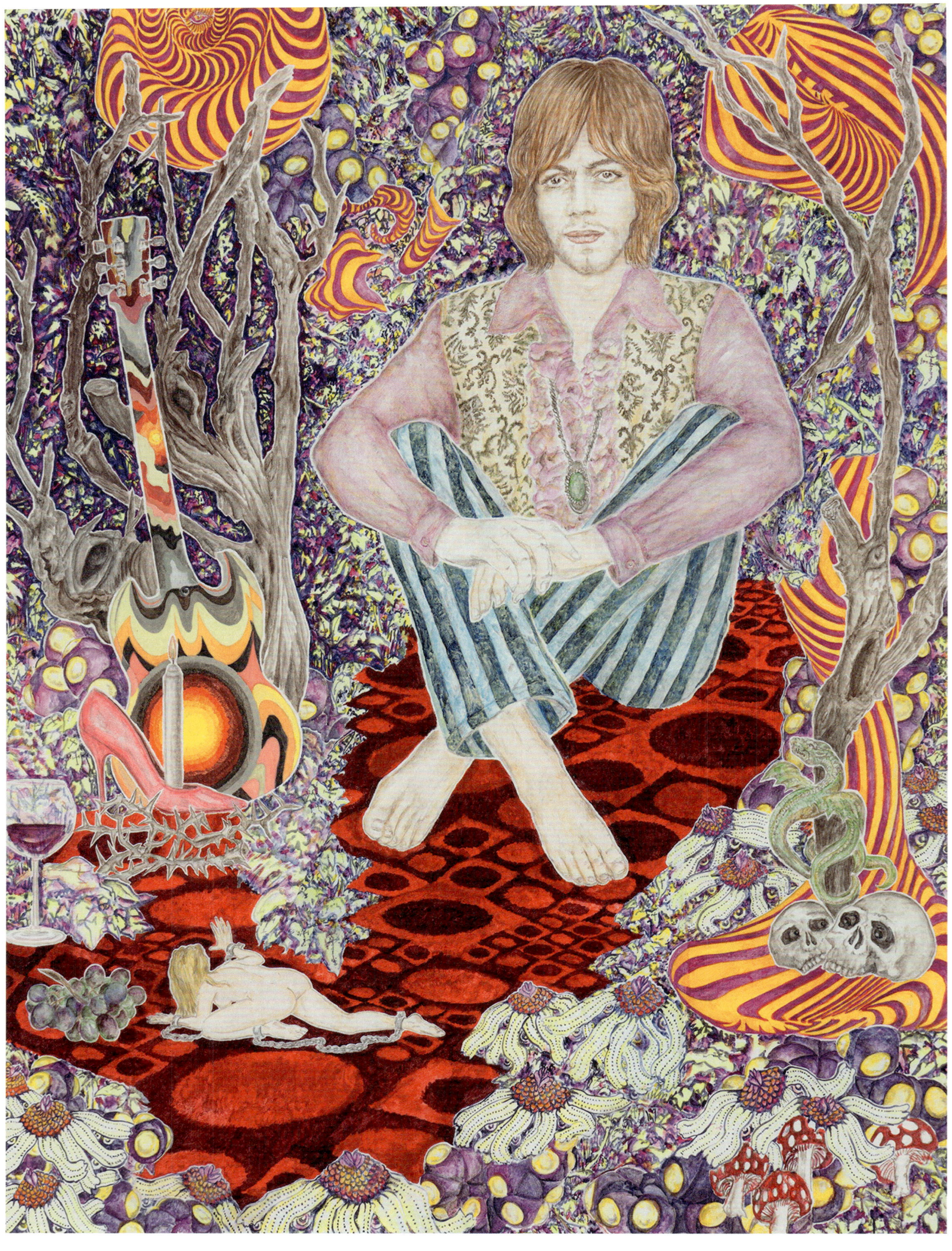

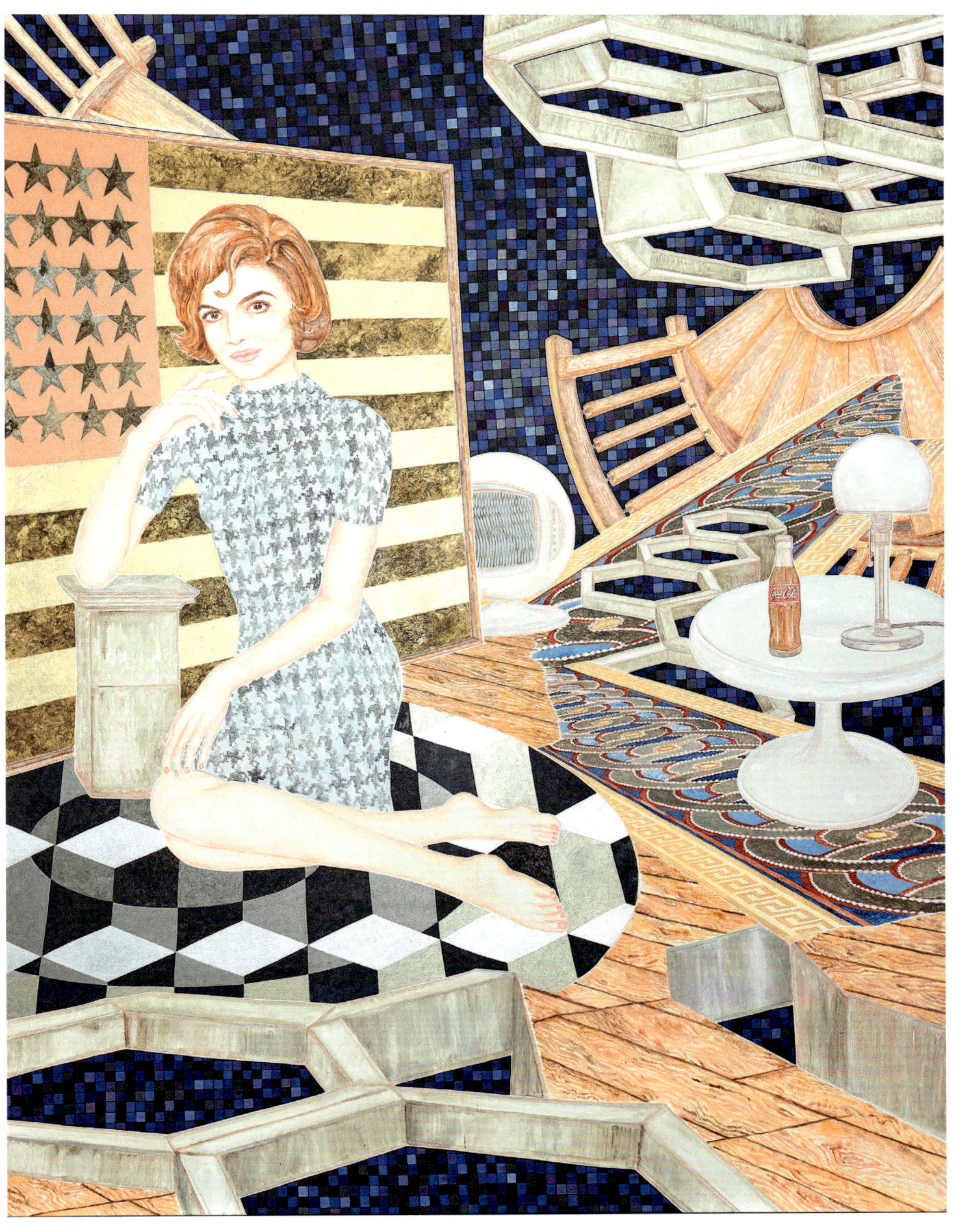
Coca-Cola

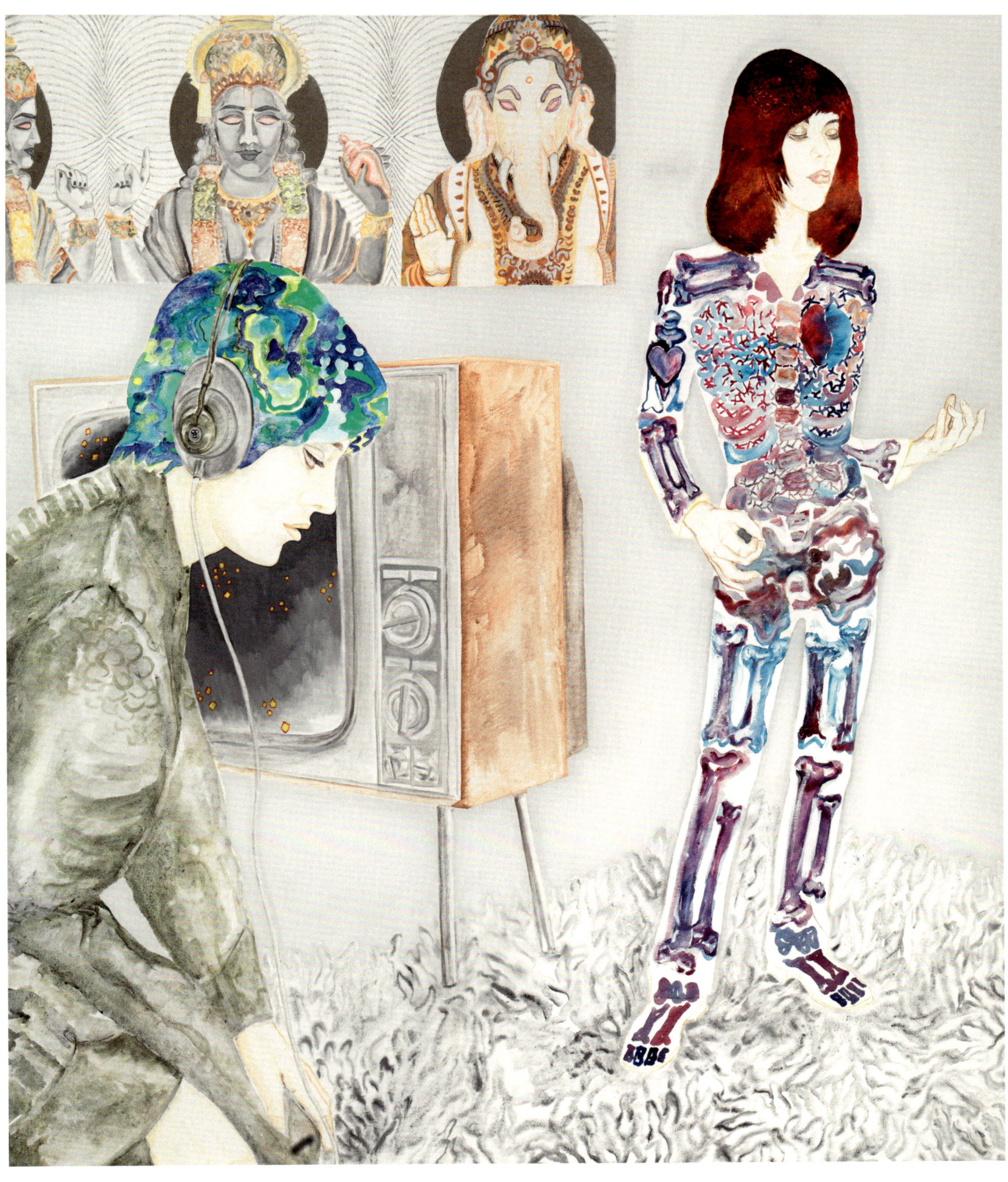

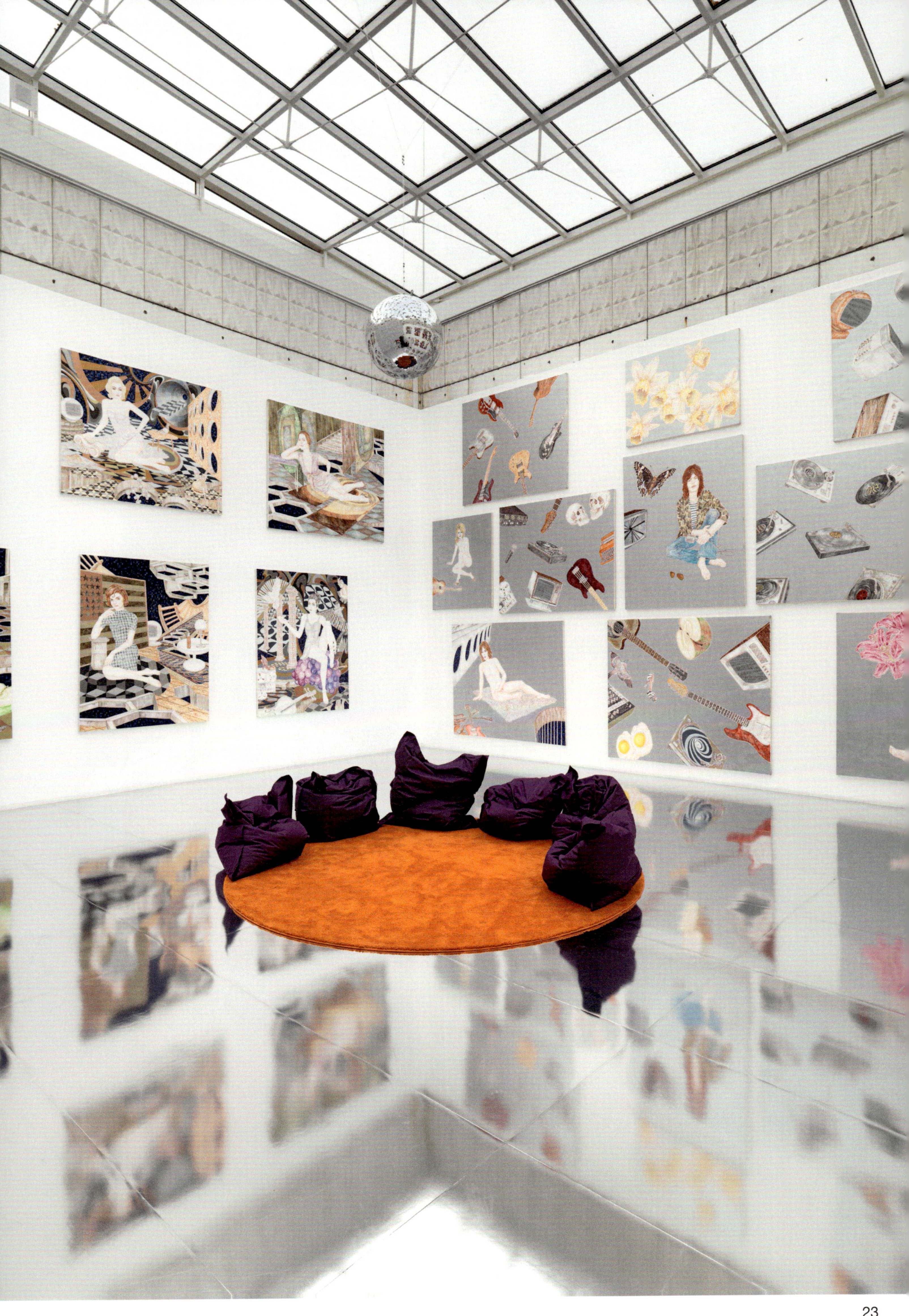

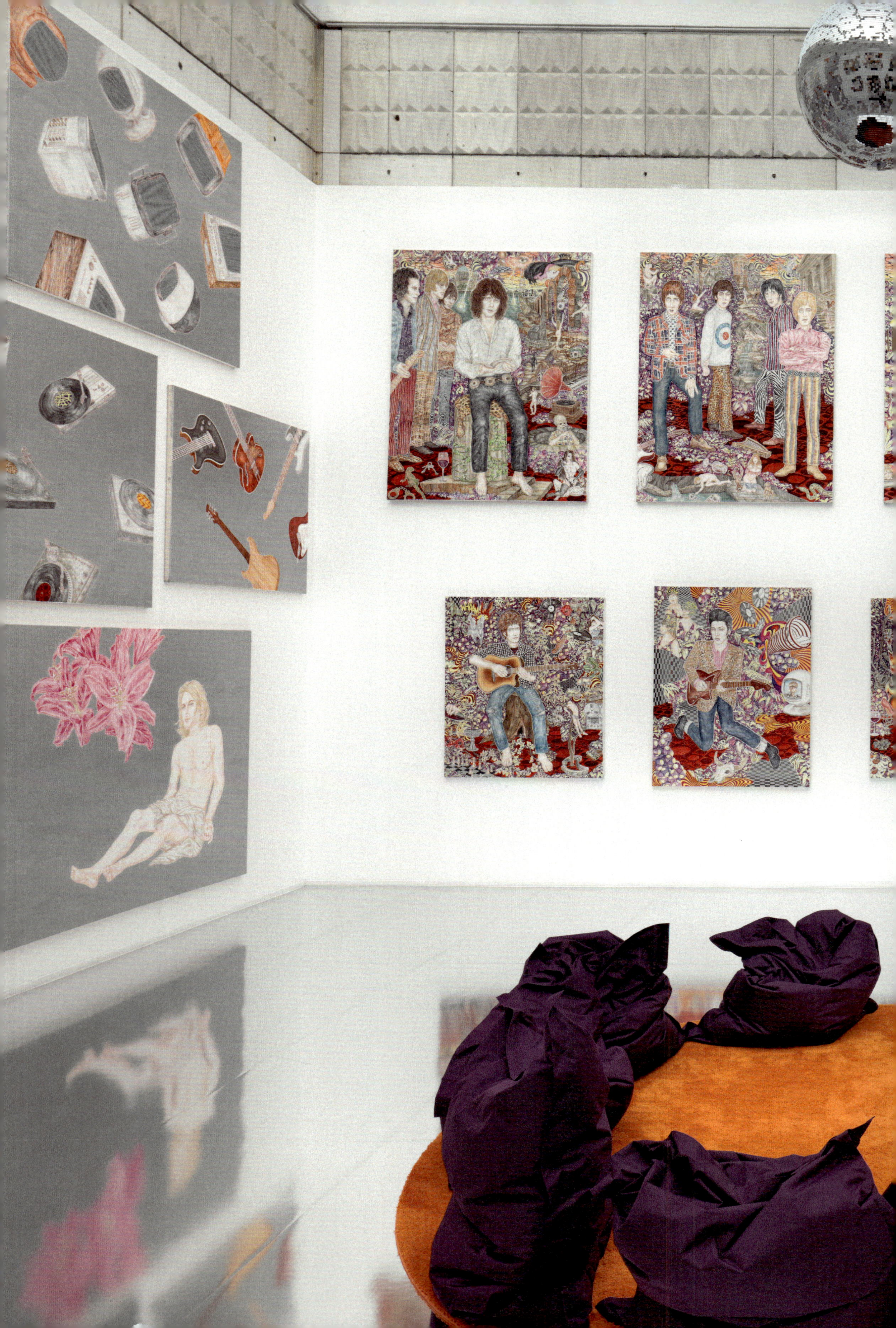

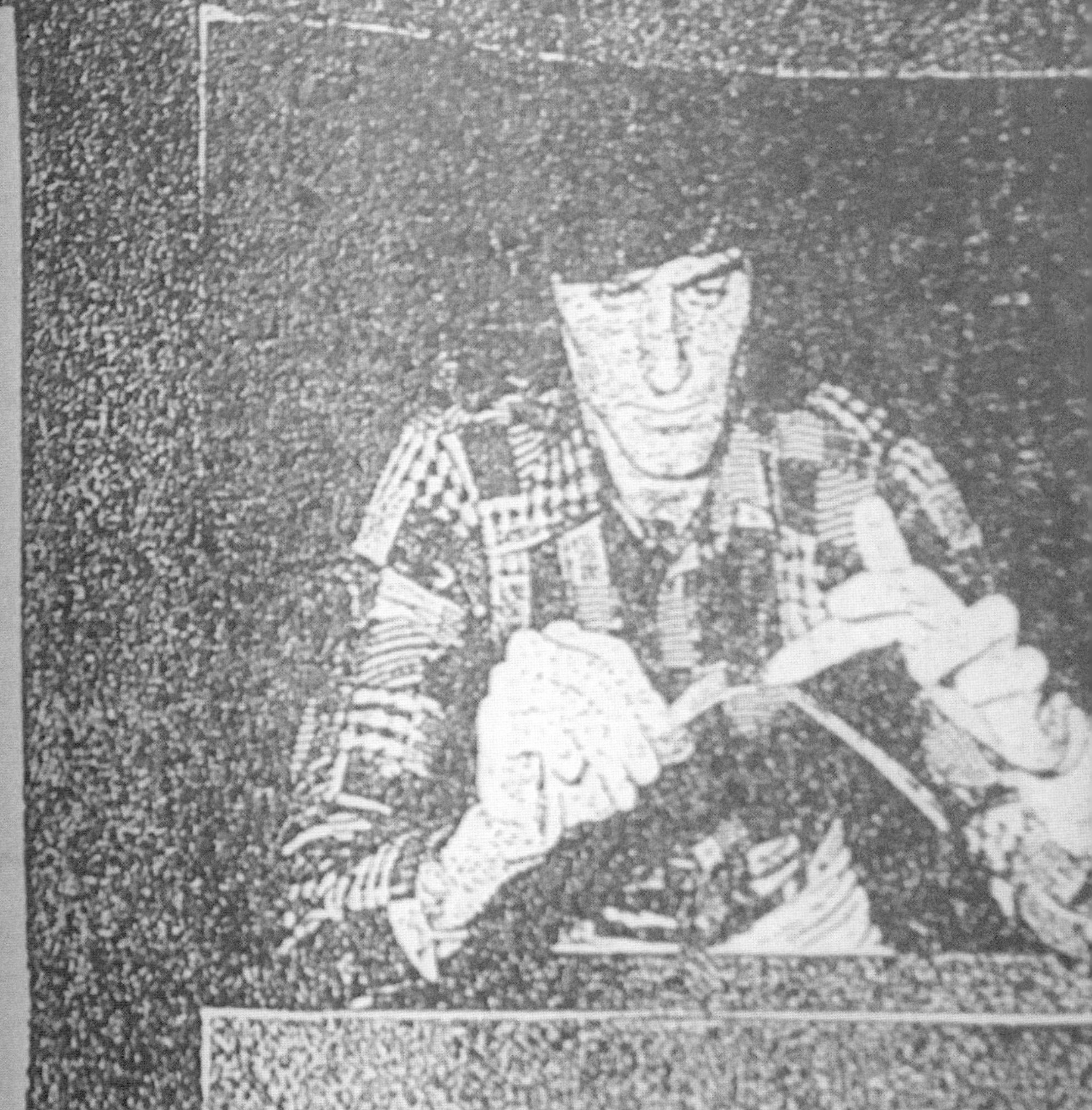

Maike Abelz.
alte
Schönhauser. 4
10119 Berlin

☎ 0177-2635058

Oliver Drescher
Torstr. 218
10115 Berlin

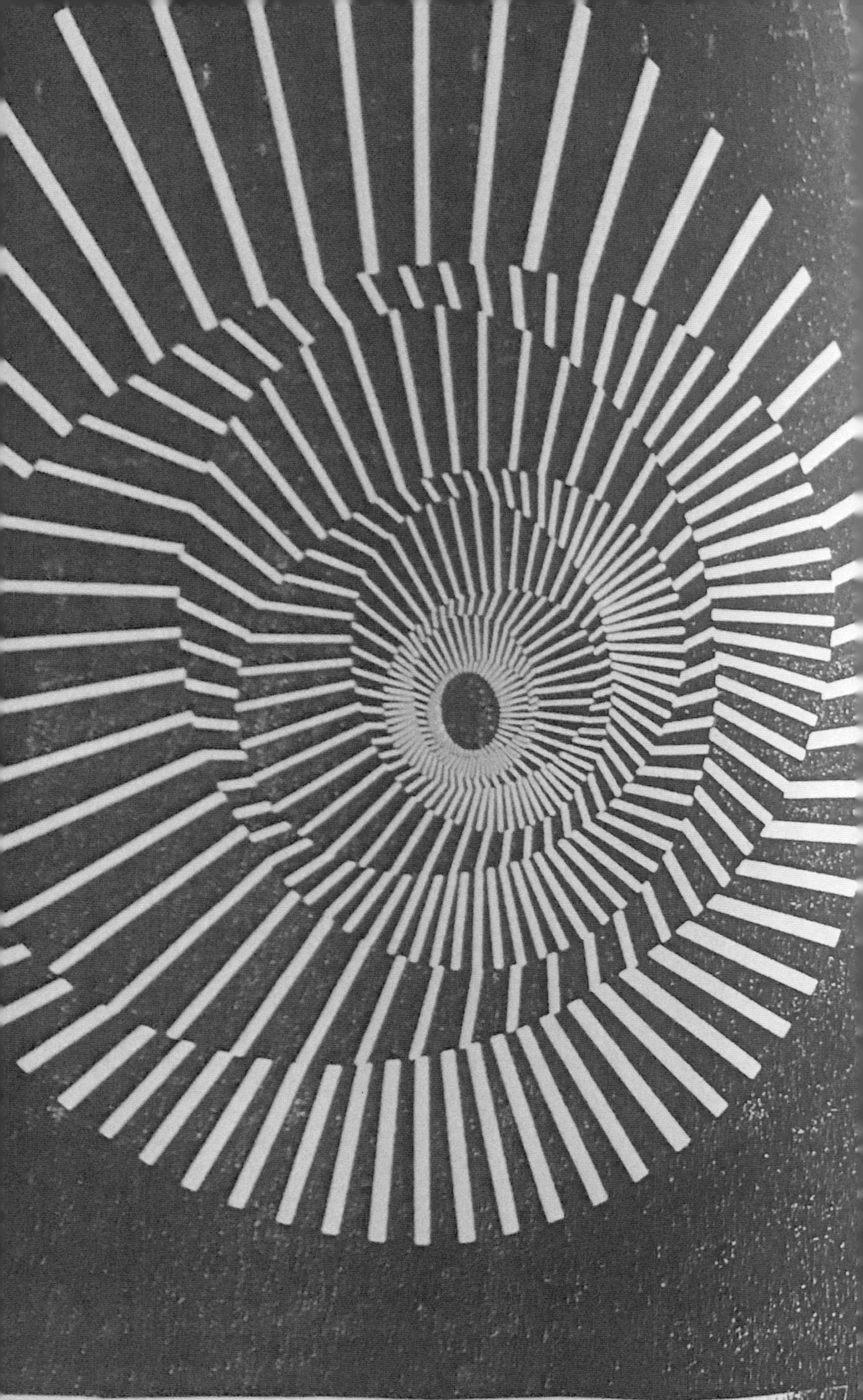

Speicherung und Übertragung

Informationen erwerben, proz

weit

Politisches Engagement

kann nicht m

Versuch sein, die Gesellschaft o

zu ändern,

sondern das soziale Relatio

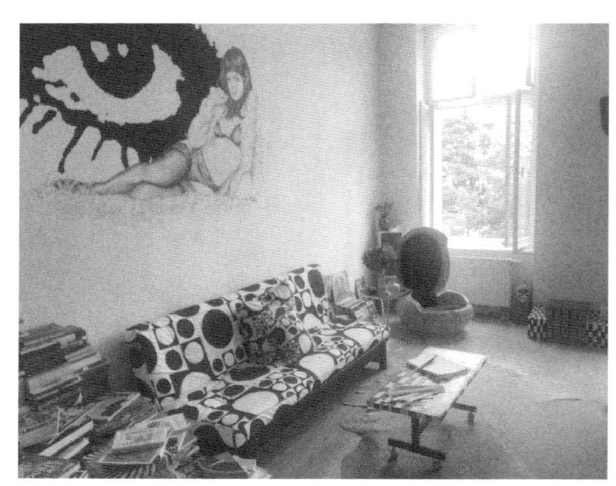

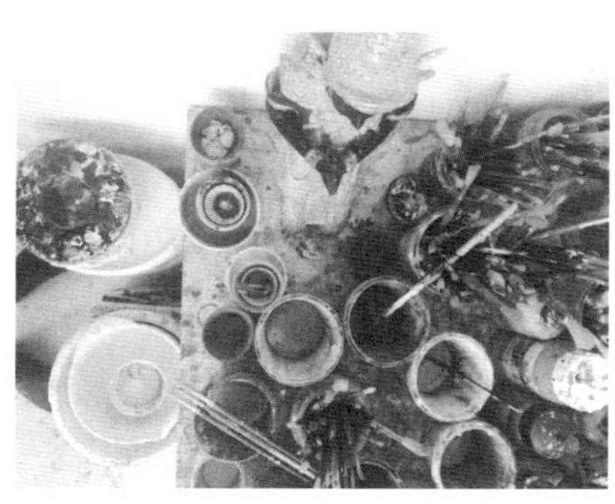

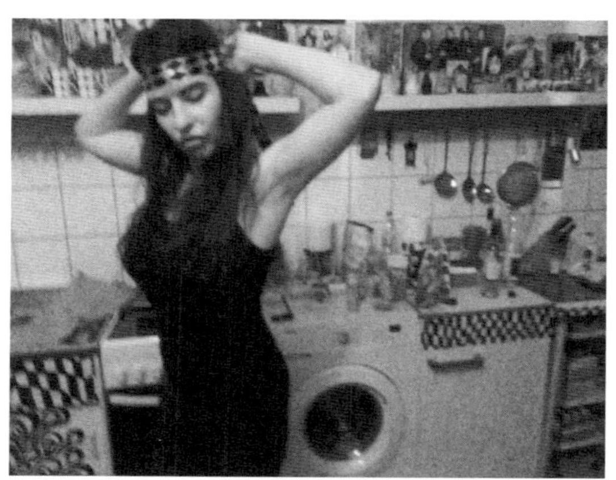

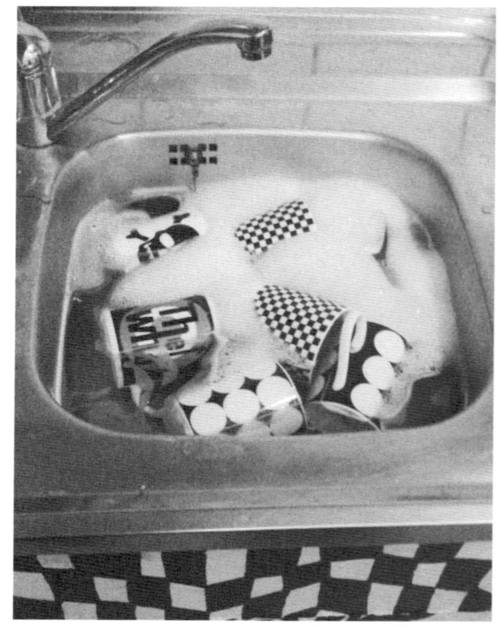

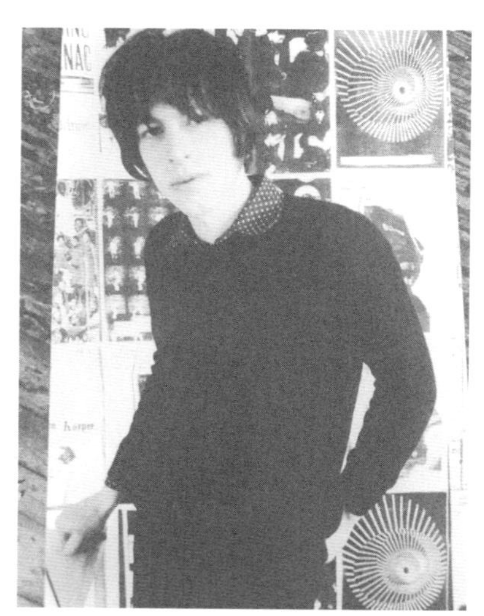

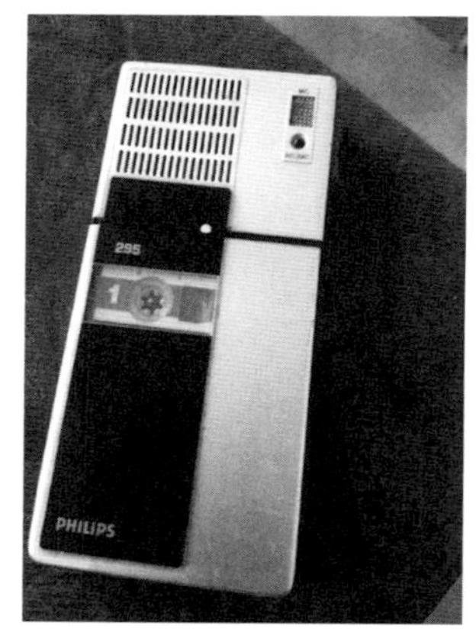
298
PHILIPS

Abetz & Drescher
Place Called Love

Diese Publikation entstand anlässlich der für die Kunsthalle Rostock konzipierten Ausstellung *Place Called Love* des in Berlin lebenden Künstlerpaars Abetz & Drescher. Sie ist ihre erste institutionelle Einzelausstellung in der seit über zwanzig Jahren gemeinsamen Schaffenszeit.

Maike Abetz und Oliver Drescher begegneten sich 1994 an der Kunstakademie Düsseldorf, wo beide in unterschiedlichen Semestern bei Alfonso Hüppi[1] studierten. 1995 zogen sie gemeinsam nach Berlin, um bis 1997 bei Katharina Sieverding an der Hochschule der Künste zu studieren. Seit 1995 agieren sie als Künstlerpaar und schaffen gemeinsame Kunstwerke unter dem Namen Abetz & Drescher. Der Neuanfang des Paars in Berlin, der parallel zur Nachwendedynamik der Stadt verlief, war entscheidend für die Ausprägung ihrer Malerkarriere, künstlerische Entwicklung und wiedererkennbare Bildsprache.

Ihre Bilder verkörpern Träume, Illusionen, Halluzination und Reflexionen der Gesellschaft am Beispiel von Aspekten der Massenkulturen, etwa aus Musik, Kunst und Science-Fiction-Filmen. Das Künstlerpaar schafft eine Symbiose, die den Zeitraum der 1960er bis zu den 1990er Jahren umfasst und Ikonen der internationalen Musik wie Mick Jagger, Jimi Hendrix, Bob Dylan, Eric Clapton und The Who einschließt. Diese sind in malerischen Darstellungen verewigt und werden dabei von ihren Instrumenten und nicht selten von den Künstlern selbst begleitet, die häufig als Protagonistin und Protagonist der eigenen Narrative in Szene gesetzt sind.

Das Ergebnis entspricht der Wiedergabe eines dynamischen, vielfältigen, lebendigen Szenariums, eingetaucht in eine psychedelische Welt der Massenkultur wie in eine Reise in die Vergangenheit, die Themen der Gegenwart und Zukunft einbeziehen. Diese entspricht der Ideologie und Lebensweise von Abetz & Drescher, die die Musik als Zentralfigur ihrer Werke wie auch als einen Leitfaden und als Spiegelung der Gesellschaft betrachten.

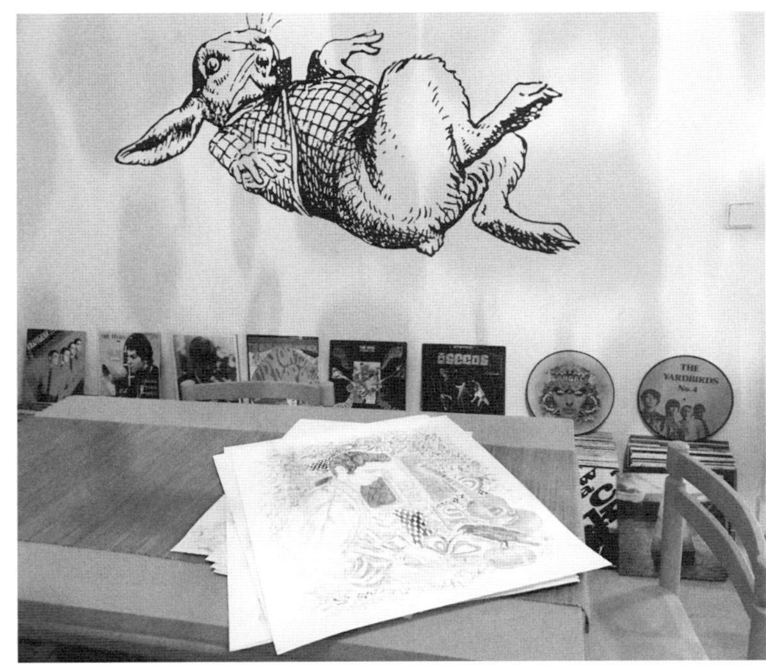

Inszenierung als Gesamtkunstwerk

Die Ausstellung *Place Called Love* verwandelt den Lichthof der Kunsthalle Rostock in ein Gesamtkunstwerk, in dem die zwischen 1997 und 2019 entstandenen Bilder von Abetz & Drescher Teil des Ganzen werden. Im geschlossenen Raum findet die Verschmelzung der Utopie, die in den Bildern zu sehen ist, statt. Die Besucherinnen und Besucher begegnen den collagenhaften, zentralen Elementen der Malerei im Raum wieder – eine einladende, farbenreich gemusterte, psychedelische Kapsel, bewohnt von Playern der Massenkultur und ihrer musikalischen Inspiration.

Der Lichthof der Kunsthalle Rostock wird Zeitzeuge seiner eigenen Verwandlung. Die Begrenzungen der Leinwände werden abgeschafft, sodass im Raum eine Einheit entsteht. Die Bilder sind die Wiedergabe einer Inszenierung – real oder imaginär bewohnt von Elementen aus dem alltäglichen Universum des Künstlerpaars. Drei Wände werden von den Bildern flankiert. Die Präsentation entspricht keiner konservativen Hängung, sondern ist in einer dichten Kombination von Themen und Serien organisiert. Die Visualisierung dieses Gesamtkunstwerks wird konkreter, indem einzelne Bestandteile der Bilder den Raum erobern. Diskokugel, verspiegelter Fußboden, bunte Teppiche, Sitzsäcke und von den Künstlern kreierte gemusterte, schwarz-weiße Tapeten im Stil der Op-Art sind im Raum platziert. Im Hintergrund hört man Lieder, die zum Repertoire von Abetz & Drescher passen.[2]

Verschiedene Elemente aus Musik, Design, Mode, Architektur und Malerei werden in einer planvollen Zusammenstellung eingefügt. Sie sind Komponenten der Malerei und lösen sich vom Bildträger, um die Ausstellungshalle zu erobern. Die ästhetischen Gebilde der Malerei beweisen sich als Bestandteil der Realität.

Die Besucherinnen und Besucher wiederum übernehmen die Rolle der Protagonistinnen und Protagonisten der Gemälde. Ihre Mimik, Gestik und Haltung werden durch diese Kulisse beeinflusst. Wie auf einer Bühne oder in einer Filmkulisse agieren sie als Darstellerinnen und Darsteller nach einem Skript, das von dem Künstlerpaar geliefert wurde: Bilder betrachten, Musik hören, sitzend entspannen und in die psychedelischen Landschaft eintauchen. Realität und Szenarium überschneiden sich, ohne dass eine Grenze sichtbar würde. Dadurch erkennt man das wahre Kunstwerk, wie Walter Benjamin erläutern würde: „Man vergleiche die Leinwand, auf der der Film abrollt, mit der Leinwand, auf der sich das Gemälde befindet. Das letztere lädt den Betrachter zur Kontemplation ein; vor ihm kann er sich seinem Assoziationsablauf überlassen. Vor der Filmaufnahme kann er das nicht. Kaum hat er sie ins Auge gefaßt, so hat sie sich schon verändert. Sie kann nicht fixiert werden.“[3] Das Erlebnis im Raum kann nicht unter den physischen oder psychischen Erlebnissen fixiert werden, da die Besucherinnen und Besucher diese Kulisse durch ihre Anwesenheit und Wahrnehmung aktivieren. Teil dieser künstlerischen Installation zu sein, bedeutet Erinnerungen und Assoziationen zu wecken.

Neugier und Hoffnung sind die Motivationsfaktoren, die dazu beitragen, dass sich Künstlerin und Betrachter in solch komplexen, künstlerischen Kontexten begegnen. Die Dynamik ist ähnlich derjenigen beim Konsum von Waren, aber der Inhalt und das Ergebnis einer intensiven kulturellen Begegnung bereichern das Ego eben nicht wie trivial konsumierte Waren: „Der Konsum von Kunst und Produkten anderer kreativer Tätigkeiten – Literatur, Philosophie, Wissenschaft und alles, was sich dazwischen befindet –, also der Konsum von Produkten der Kreativität anderer Menschen, birgt in sich immer etwas Unerwartetes, Neues, Überraschendes, etwas, was ein konkret vorhandenes Bedürfnis überschreitet. Dadurch aber kommt es – wie paradox das auch klingen mag – zur Befriedigung des speziellen Bedürfnisses nach Neuem, nach Erweiterung des Bestehenden, nach der Auseinandersetzung mit dem Unbekannten, kurz des Bedürfnisses nach innerer Erneuerung des Konsumierenden. Der Konsument sucht nicht – oder sucht nicht in erster Linie – nur die Bestätigung seiner selbst.“[4] Nicht nur eine Künstlerin ist ein engagierter Kunstkonsument, sondern alle, die nicht resigniert sind. *Place Called Love* ist eine Plattform, um die menschlichen Sinne und Wahrnehmung zu schärfen.

Lebenswerk des Lebenskünstlers

Maike Abetz und Oliver Drescher leben ihre Kunst, die eine treue Wiedergabe ihrer Existenz ist. Es gibt zahlreiche Künstlerpaare, die ihren Platz in der Kunstgeschichte erobert haben, wie zum Beispiel Gilbert and George,[5] Christo und Jeanne-Claude,[6] Eva und Adele,[7] Bernd und Hilla Becher,[8] Elmgreen & Dragset[9] und Fischli/Weiss,[10] und die ihre Projekte nur als Paar – als Ergebnis einer Symbiose – konzipieren und realisieren. Und sich auch – ähnlich wie Abetz & Drescher – mit der Malerei beschäftigen, wie Römer & Römer.[11] Zahlreiche Ausstellungen haben das Thema des Künstlerpaars oder Künstlerduos in den Fokus gesetzt,[12] um zu unterscheiden, ob sie jeweils ihre eigene künstlerische Laufbahn verfolgen oder, wie bei Abetz & Drescher, ein gemeinsames künstlerisches Werk schaffen. Dieses Künstlerdasein weckt mehrere Fragen: „ … kreativer Austausch oder Einfluss? Rivalität? Selbstbestimmung des weiblichen Partners? Künstlerische und persönliche Harmonie?“[13]

Abetz & Drescher betonen, dass es bei ihrer Begegnung ein natürliches Interesse an gemeinsamen Themen und an einer Lebensart gab, wie auch der Drang, etwas Neues für sich als eine Bereicherung für beide zu erfinden.[14] Maike Abetz hatte von Beginn an ein großes Interesse für die Malerei und fokussierte sich intensiv auf Bildmerkmale und ihre eigenen Vorbilder. Euphorisch erzählt sie, dass der 2010 verstorbene Maler Sigmar Polke und besonders sein ikonisches Werk *Höhere Wesen befahlen: rechte obere Ecke schwarz malen!,*[15] das vor genau fünfzig Jahren entstand, ihre künstlerische Praxis beeinflusst hat. Die Banalität des Titels, des Motivs (schwarzes Dreieck auf weißem Grund) und sogar der banale Reim (befahlen – malen) könnten Hinweise auf spirituelle Einflüsse sein, reine Ironie des Künstlers oder eine effektive Art und Weise zur Verteidigung einer Künstlerautonomie beim Schaffensprozess, indem er eine Ablenkung oder Ausrede findet, um dem Fokus von seiner künstlerischen Entscheidung abzulenken. Nicht nur Polkes Haltung hat Abetz’ Aufmerksamkeit erregt, sondern auch die Art und Weise, wie er seine Leinwände und Bilder im Allgemeinen komponiert hat: „Insbesondere Sigmar Polkes Bilder seien zahlreiche Spuren einer sich im Wandel befindlichen Gesellschaft: Triviale Szenen, Banalitäten des alltäglichen Lebens, kleinbürgerliche Ambitionen, nationale und internationale Politik – diese Themen zerlegte er unter der Lupe seiner schonungslosen Analyse. Geliefert hat er dabei eine einmalige Version der Realität, die von Ironie, Humor und Kritik durchsetzt ist. Seine Alchemie kombiniert sich aus Intuition, Planung und Zufall und auch das Materielle trug seinen Teil dazu bei. Experimentelle Neugierde war schon immer einer seiner Wesenszüge. Sie war es auch, die ihn dazu trieb, sämtliche verfügbare Techniken und Genres zu bespielen: Malerei, Zeichnung, Gouache, Fotografie, Objektkunst, Filme und Editionen.“[16]

Währenddessen sind die Interessen von Oliver Drescher hauptsächlich in der Philosophie verankert: „Unter den Philosophen sind es vor allem die französischen wie Michel Foucault, Roland Barthes, Paul Virilio, Gilles Deleuze. Aber auch sehr wichtig ist der deutsche Medientheoretiker Friedrich Kittler. Bei ihm habe ich auch studiert. Bildhauer wären die aus den 1960er Jahren zu nennen: Claes Oldenburg, James Rosenquist, Jasper Johns, Tom Wesselmann, George Segal. Aber auch sehr wichtig: Martin Kippenberger und Mike Kelley.“[17] Sein Schwerpunkt ist immer, über den Inhalt nachzudenken, nachzufragen und zu strukturieren. Er interessierte sich zu Anfang seiner Studienzeit für Bildhauerei, die für ihn die Gedanken in konkrete Gestalten verwandeln kann.

Doch die Symbiose zwischen Maike Abetz und Oliver Drescher kristallisiert sich schließlich in der Malerei heraus. Die Verwendung von Acrylfarbe auf großen Leinwänden entspricht der Verschmelzung beider Künstler – ihr Interesse, ihre Malweise, ästhetische und inhaltliche Auseinandersetzungen werden unter der Signatur Abetz & Drescher zusammengefasst, ohne Spuren der Einzelidentitäten für die Betrachtenden zu hinterlassen. Ihre Werke entsprechen dem Spirit der Berliner Kunstszene Mitte der 1990er Jahre und finden große Resonanz als Bestandteil der neuen deutschen Malerei: „Die prallbunte Malerei von Maike Abetz und Oliver Drescher scheint auf den ersten Blick in farbdrastischem Sixties-Revival zu baden, versammelt in psychedelischen Bildräumen überwiegend Vertreter der schon etwas angejahrten Popkultur, hier gleichwohl im besten ‚Viva'-Alter porträtiert. Doch die Verflechtungen reichen weiter, antike Götter und barocke Putten sind ebenso vertreten wie altgriechische Bogenarchitektur, die plötzlich in Op-Art-Ornamentik mündet. Die Bilder sind Zeitmaschinen, sie erzeugen hyperhistorische und zugleich synthetische Räume, die insbesondere das Medium Musik ins Visuelle übersetzen und kulturelle Codes zu dicht gestaffelten Allegorien binden." [18]

Das Genre des Selbstporträts ist ein großer Bestandteil ihres Œuvres, einzeln oder eingebunden in ihr Universum, das von der Musik geprägt ist. Im Stil der 1960er und 1970er Jahre werden die Protagonistinnen und Protagonisten mit den typischen Ornamenten der Zeit dargestellt. Sie sind fester Bestandteil ihrer Selbstdarstellung, Inszenierung und Wahrnehmung. Ein Mitstreiter der Selbstinszenierung war Martin Kippenberger, der die eigene Rolle immer wieder kritisch oder ironisch dargestellt und hinterfragt hat. Seine erste Einzelausstellung im Jahr 1981 in der nGbK (neue Gesellschaft für bildende Kunst, Berlin) hieß *Lieber Maler, male mir* ... Es war ein ironischer Hinweis auf die Rolle des Künstlers/Malers und seine Selbstdarstellung in der Malerei: „Der Titel Kippenbergers ist als radikales Statement über die Stellung des Künstlers von heute zu sehen. Man sollte die Aufforderung wörtlich verstehen: ‚Lieber Maler, male mir' bzw. ‚Lieber Maler, male mir etwas'. Kippenberger delegiert nicht nur auf sarkastische Weise die künstlerische Verantwortung, sondern betont auch unmissverständlich, dass die ‚liebe' Figur des Malers seine kulturelle Allgemeingültigkeit verloren hat." [19] Diese kritische Aussage entstand u. a. deswegen, weil die Serie von zwölf Bildern, die Martin Kippenberger in der Ausstellung präsentiert hat, das Ergebnis eines dafür beauftragten Kinoplakatmalers war. Seine Aufgabe war es, den Künstler in den Plakatmotiven in seiner Künstlerrolle nachzuahmen.

Zusätzlich zum Selbstporträt ist die figurative Malerei von Abetz & Drescher immer von zwei zentralen Figuren bewohnt: die Künstlerin und der Künstler selbst, die eventuell gegenseitig füreinander posieren wie etwa bei den Arbeiten *Atmosphères* (2000) oder *Up Against It* (1997); weibliche Musen als Diva und Pin-Up-Gestalt oder Musikerinnen und Musiker, die die Inspiration für das künstlerische Schaffen durch ihre Lieder liefern. Die Hommage wird im Titel der Bilder betont: Maria Callas, Jimi Hendrix, Mick Jagger, The Who, The Doors, Elvis Presley – zahlreiche Mythen werden mit diesen Personen und Titeln zelebriert.

Die Farbpalette verhält sich authentisch zu den legendären Vintage-Bilder in einer Kombination von orange, rot, pink, blau, silber. Die Hauptfiguren – besonders bei der „Musikerserie" – werden vor einen lebendigen Hintergrund platziert, dessen gesamte Fläche Teil des Narrativs ist. Einzelne Szenen vermischen sich und der Effekt des Bild-im-Bild hypnotisiert die Betrachtenden. Die Aufmerksamkeit wird auf die magische, zeichnerische Darstellung der Mythen gelenkt. Die Augen flanieren unruhig in einer dichten, konstruierten Landschaft mit Tieren, Menschen, Pflanzen, Spielen, Genüssen und allen Sorten von Exzessen des Lebens bis hin zur Darstellung von Totenköpfen. Diese intensiven, surrealistischen Kompositionen erinnern an Wiedergaben halluzinogener Experimente, zum Beispiel in den Werken *Mick Jagger*, *The Doors*, *Eric Clapton*, die 2011 entstanden sind.

In aktuellen Werken, die ab 2017 entstanden sind, werden weibliche Darstellungen gefeiert, indem sie als Einzelpersonen zentriert im Bild präsentiert werden. Ihre Haltungen sind souverän, sublim. Ihre Mimiken und Gestiken laden die Betrachtenden zum direkten Dialog ein. Sie befinden sich sitzend in Innenräumen, die wie Raumkapseln wirken. Diese sind mit optischen Mustern ausgestaltet, die die Illusion einer tiefen Perspektive schaffen. Räume wie diejenigen der Bilder *Rebirth*, *Answer My Prayer* und *Flashback* ermöglichen durch verschiedene Öffnungen eine Betrachtung der Außenwelt. Wie in einem Raumschiff umkreist die Muse das Universum, als wäre sie für Menschen unantastbar.

Nun werden bei den jüngsten Werken die Einzelelemente gelöst und extrahiert. Plattenspieler oder Gitarren schweben vor silbernen, monochromatischen Hintergründen wie in *Supernature*, *Soul Explosion* oder *Stardust* (alle 2019). Abetz & Drescher bleiben ihren Ikonen und ihren Spuren treu. Sie schaffen ein authentisches Lebenswerk am Beispiel der Lebenskünstlerinnen und -künstler, die sie in ihrer Malerei vergöttern und verewigen.

Mythos der Popkultur

San Francisco war schon in den 1950er Jahren Bühne der Beat-Generation. Die Protagonisten waren Dichter und Schriftsteller, die zusammen mit bildenden Künstlern wie Bruce Conner[20] eine neue Ästhetik und Programmatik mit einem kritischen Blick auf gesellschaftliche Strömungen verteidigten. Vor fünfzig Jahren fand das legendäre *Woodstock* Festival statt. 32 Bands und Solokünstler traten vor geschätzten 400.000 Besuchern auf. Das Festival war zwar eine kommerziell unkoordinierte Veranstaltung, gleichwohl verkörperte es in einer kontroversen politischen, sozialen und ökonomischen Zeit die Sehnsucht nach Love & Peace.

In den 1960er Jahren stand die Gegenkultur auf der internationalen Tagesordnung. Die künstlerischen Bewegungen, angeführt von bildenden Künstlern, Schriftstellerinnen, Filmemachern, Modedesignerinnen und Musikern, verteidigten das Recht auf Gleichheit in der Gesellschaft, unabhängig vom sozioökonomischen Hintergrund.

Es wurde zu einem historischen Wahrzeichen der Massenbewegungen für Proteste, die bis in die Gegenwart Teil der zeitgenössischen, soziopolitischen Agenda sind: „Die 1960er Jahre werden zumeist im Zusammenhang mit der Revolution diskutiert. Während des gesamten Jahrzehnts und auf der ganzen Welt wurde eine Generation junger Menschen aktiv und bewirkte eine Reihe sozialer und politischer Transformationen. Die daraus entstandene staatliche Politik beförderte fünfzig Jahre später im Westen einen Lebensstil, der für niemanden außer den überzeugtesten Visionären der 1960er Jahre vorstellbar gewesen wäre. Auch ein ästhetisches Erbe dieser Zeit dauert an und zeigt sich am stärksten in der Modewelt, in der der sogenannte ‚Bohemian-Chic' nach wie vor besteht und Erinnerungen an einen turbulenten, aber hoffnungsvollen Abschnitt amerikanischer Geschichte heraufbeschwört. Intellektuelle, Philosophen und Dichter dieser Zeit haben immer mehr Beweise dafür geliefert, dass ein Wandel auf allen gesellschaftlichen Ebenen nicht nur möglich, sondern grundsätzlich erstrebenswert ist."[21]

Die Bewegung der 1960er Jahre prägte und inspirierte Abetz & Drescher und ist bis heute entscheidend für ihre künstlerische Entwicklung und ihr Schaffen. Die Realisierung ihrer Ausstellung *Place Called Love* in der Kunsthalle Rostock offenbart, dass bestimmte Themen, Auseinandersetzungen und Kontexte noch im Jubiläumsjahr vom „Summer of Love" präsent sind. Parallel dazu ist es ein glücklicher Zufall, dass auch die Kunsthalle Rostock im Jahr 2019 ihr fünfzigstes Jubiläum zelebriert. Der einzige Museumsneubau der DDR wurde 1969 eröffnet. Durch diese Ausstellung bringen wir so zwei unterschiedliche Kontexte in einen Dialog, die simultan existieren – auf der einen Seite die Spuren der Popkultur, die in den 1960er Jahren im Westen entstanden ist, und auf der anderen Seite eine kulturelle Plattform aus dem ehemaligen „Ost-Block", die bis heute ihre Rolle als Vermittler von soziokulturellen Kontexten wahrnimmt.

Tereza de Arruda, Kuratorin

1 Alfonso Hüppi (geb. 1935 in Freiburg im Breisgau) ist ein Schweizer Maler, Grafiker und Bildhauer. Er lebt in Baden-Baden und zeitweise in Namibia. Zwischen 1974 und 1999 war er Professor für Malerei an der Kunstakademie Düsseldorf.

2 Darunter u. a. Klassiker von Jimi Hendrix (*Voodoo Child*, *All Along the Watchtower*, *Third Stone from the Sun*), The Doors (*Light My Fire*, *Break On Through [To the Other Side]*), The Rolling Stones (*Paint It Black*, *Sympathy for the Devil*), Daft Punk (*Da Funk*), Cream (*White Room*), Aretha Franklin (*Think*, *Respect*), Elvis Presley (*Shake, Rattle and Roll*, *Blue Suede Shoes*), The Seeds (*Pictures and Design*), Bob Dylan (*Subterranean Homesick Blues*), Nirvana (*Smells Like Teen Spirit*), Brigitte Bardot (*Ça pourrait changer*), Barn Owl (*Devotion II*, *The Darkest Night Since 1683*), Acid Jesus (*Jesus*), The Supremes (*I Hear a Symphony*), Curtis Mayfield (*Move On Up*).

3 Walter Benjamin, *Das Kunstwerk im Zeitalter seiner technischen Reproduzierbarkeit*, Frankfurt/Main 1977, S. 38.

4 Jan Kotik, „Kunst, Kitsch und Design", in: Harry Pross (Hg.), *Kitsch. Soziale und politische Aspekte einer Geschmacksfrage*, München 1985, S. 137.

5 Gilbert Prousch (geb. 1943 in St. Martin in Thurn, Italien) und George Passmore (geb. 1942 in Plymouth, Großbritannien).

6 Christo Wladimirow Jawaschew (geb. 1935 in Gabrowo, Bulgarien) und Jeanne-Claude (geb. 1935 als Jeanne-Claude Denat de Guillebon in Casablanca, Französisch-Marokko; gest. 2009 in New York City, US).

7 Das Künstlerpaar Eva und Adele ersetzt biografische Angaben mit den Zahlen zu Körpergröße, Oberweite, Taille und Hüfte, vgl. https://de.wikipedia.org/wiki/Eva_%26_Adele#Biographie, abgerufen am 5.11.2019.

8 Bernd Becher (eigentlich Bernhard Becher, geb. 1931 in Siegen; gest. 2007 in Rostock) und Hilla Becher (geb. 1934 als Hilla Wobeser in Potsdam; gest. 2015 in Düsseldorf).

9 Michael Elmgreen (geb. 1961 in Kopenhagen, Dänemark) und Ingar Dragset (geb. 1969 in Trondheim, Norwegen).

10 Peter Fischli (geb. 1952 in Zürich, Schweiz) und David Weiss (geb. 1946 in Zürich, Schweiz; gest. 2012 in Zürich, Schweiz).

11 Torsten Römer (geb. 1968 in Aachen) und Nina Römer (geb. 1978 als Nina Tangian in Moskau, Russland).

12 Vgl. u. a. *Künstlerpaare: Liebe, Kunst und Leidenschaft,* Wallraf-Richartz-Museum & Fondation Corboud, Köln 31.10.2008–8.2.2009, und Gemeentemuseum, Den Haag 21.2. – 1.6.2009; *Artist Lovers,* Liverpool Biennial. 24.9.1999–7.11.1999.

13 Konstanze Crüwell, „Künstlerpaare: In jedem Fall sind die Partner vernichtet", *Frankfurter Allgemeine Zeitung,* 6.1.2009. https://www.faz.net/aktuell/feuilleton/kunst/kuenstlerpaare-in-jedem-fall-sind-die-partner-vernichtet-1591578.html, abgerufen am 5.11.2019.

14 Beim Gespräch im Künstleratelier in Berlin am 17.10.2019.

15 *Höhere Wesen befahlen: rechte obere Ecke schwarz malen!* 1969, synthetische Farbe auf Leinwand, 151,2 x 126,1 x 3 cm, 165 x 139 x 11 cm (mit Rahmen), Sammlung The Van Abbemuseum Collection, gekauft 1977, Inventarnummer 767.

16 Tereza de Arruda, *Sigmar Polke. The Editions*, me Collectors room Berlin / Stiftung Olbricht, Köln 2017, S. 34.

17 Beim Gespräch im Künstleratelier in Berlin am 17.10.2019.

18 Christoph Tannert, *Neue Deutsche Malerei,* München, Berlin, London, New York 2007, S. 67.

19 Alison M. Gingeras, „Lieber Maler, male mir …", in: *„Lieber Maler, male mir …". Radikaler Realismus nach Picabia*, Ausst.-Kat., Centre Pompidou, Paris; Kunsthalle Wien, Wien; Schirn Kunsthalle, Frankfurt/Main 2002, S. 9.

20 Bruce Conner (geb. 1933 in McPherson, Kansas, US; gest. 2008 in San Francisco, US).

21 Jill D'Alessandro, Colleen Terry, „What are we fighting for", in: *The Summer of Love. Art, Fashion, and Rock and Roll,* Ausst.-Kat., Fine Arts Museums of San Francisco, University of California Press, Berkeley 2017, S. 271.

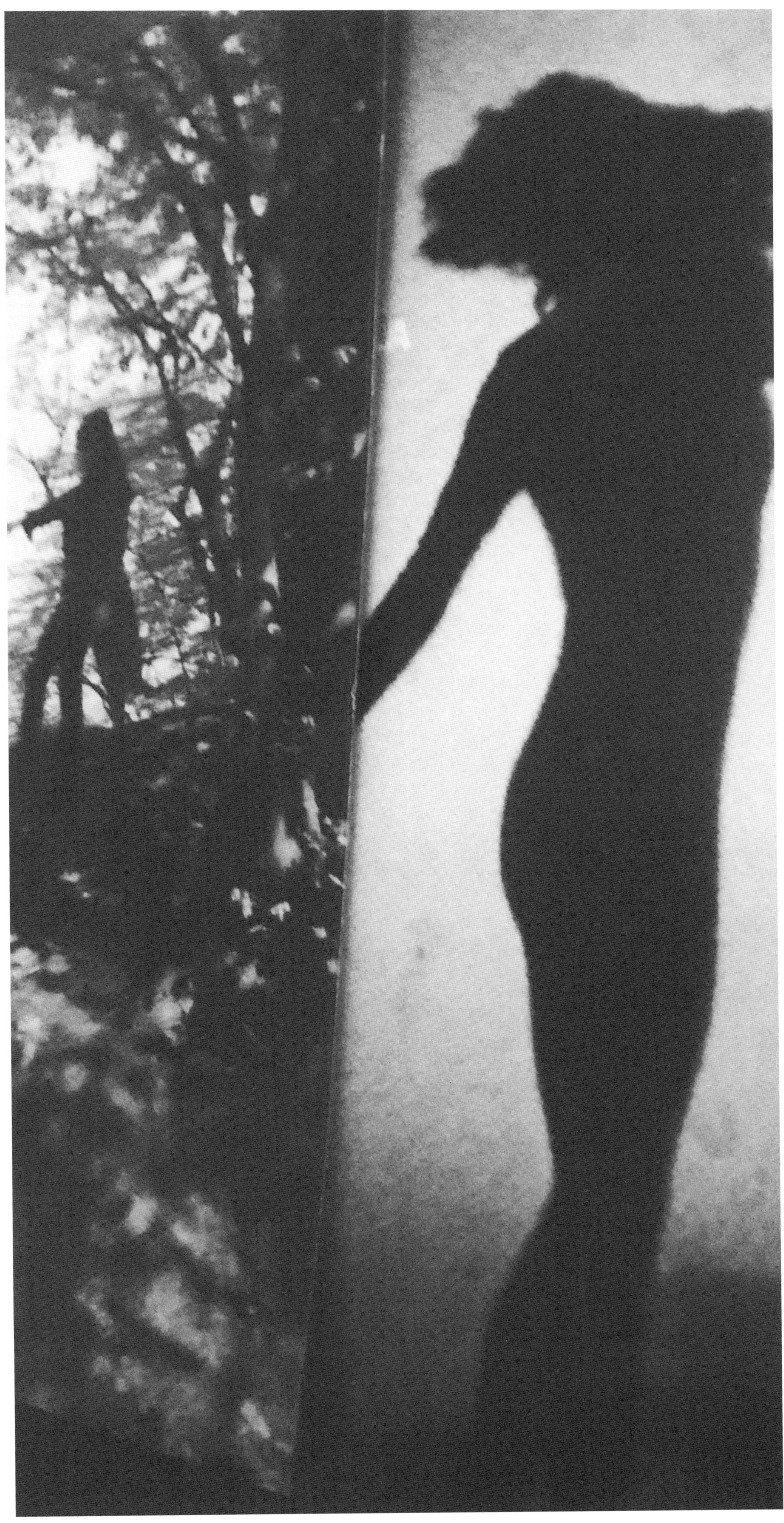

Interview Tereza de Arruda und Abetz & Drescher

T.A.: Eure erste Begegnung fand 1994 in der Kunstakademie Düsseldorf statt. Ab wann habt ihr entschieden, als Künstlerduo zu arbeiten oder sozusagen zu existieren – da diese Entscheidung eure komplette Existenz beeinflusst? War es die Thematik oder die Malweise eurer Werke, die euch dazu gebracht hat?

A&D: Kennengelernt haben wir uns an der Kunstakademie in Düsseldorf am 7.12.1994, auf einer Party. Seitdem sind wir ein Paar. Die Zusammenarbeit hat sich aus unserem Wunsch heraus entwickelt, in die Kunst einzubringen, was wir beide zu dieser Zeit in der Kunst vermisst haben. Als wir uns kennenlernten, hat Oliver Bildhauerei studiert und Maike Malerei. Wir wollten die Malerei der 1980er Jahre überwinden und ein Konzept für eine neue Malerei entwickeln. Für uns war noch nicht alles gemalt worden, im Gegenteil, wir haben festgestellt, dass noch nichts gemalt worden ist.

T.A.: Die Popkultur spielt eine große Rolle in eurer künstlerischen Darstellung – sei es Musik, Mode oder Design. Geht es bei eurer Auseinandersetzung mit diesen Elementen um den Inhalt oder um die ästhetischen Komponenten?

A&D: Wir wollten die Grenzen aufheben und öffnen zwischen Malerei, Mode, Musik, Design, Medien, Architektur, Philosophie und (Geo)Politik. Unsere Gemälde sind Bilder über Bilder über Bilder.
Kunst bedeutet ein Zeichen zu setzen.
Es ist ein magischer Akt. Es ging uns um Identitätsbildung unter medientechnischen Bedingungen und um Speicherung und Übertragung.

T.A.: Eure Bilder tragen ein klares, subjektives und figuratives Narrativ. Die Darstellungen und Haltungen der weiblichen und männlichen Protagonisten in den Bildern sind Nachahmungen ihres Universums. Wie wichtig ist es für euch, das eigene Bild und das Dasein zu inszenieren? Welche Rolle spielt das Genderthema in diesem Kontext?

A&D: Das Genderthema und ein Aufbrechen der Geschlechterstereotypen war uns sehr wichtig.
Zu nennen ist da Judith Butler, die die Gendertheorie angestoßen hat. Judith Butler ist beeinflusst von Michel Foucault und Jacques Lacan, welcher ja bekanntlich in den Zirkeln der Surrealisten involviert war. Wir wollen die Autorenschaft aufheben.

T.A.: Der Mensch ist in der Regel das Produkt seiner persönlichen und gesellschaftlichen Beziehungen. Eure Werke sind das Produkt ihrer persönlichen und gesellschaftlichen Beziehungen. Ohne persönliche und gesellschaftliche Beziehungen tendiert der Mensch zum Verlust seiner authentischen Menschlichkeit. Wie könnt ihr eure Werke als Verkörperung dieser persönlichen Symbiose erklären?

A&D: Es ging uns um das Herstellen künstlicher Identitäten. Informationen erwerben, prozessieren und weitergeben. Bilder machen fordert, das subjektiv Ersehene ins Intersubjektive zu übersetzen, in ein kollektives Relationsfeld zu tauchen. Wir wollten die Popkultur und Rock'n'Roll zu Protagonisten der Kunst machen.

T.A.: Die erste Solo-Ausstellung von Martin Kippenberger im Jahr 1981 an der nGbK (neue Gesellschaft für bildende Kunst, Berlin) hieß *Lieber Maler, male mir …* Es war ein ironischer Hinweis auf die Rolle des Künstlers/Malers. Was bedeutet für euch die Selbstdarstellung in eurer Malerei?

A&D: Eine Tendenz der Kunst ist die Aufhebung des Unterschieds zwischen Leben und Kunst. Uns geht es um diese Aufhebung – für uns gibt es keine High oder Low Culture. Somit schafft Kunst Beziehungen, die zu einer authentischen Menschlichkeit führt. Wir sind Protagonisten unserer eigenen Bilderwelt. Den Weg von den Alten Griechen über die Renaissance, von der Romantik über die 1920er Jahre hin zu den 60's reflektieren wir in unseren Bildern.

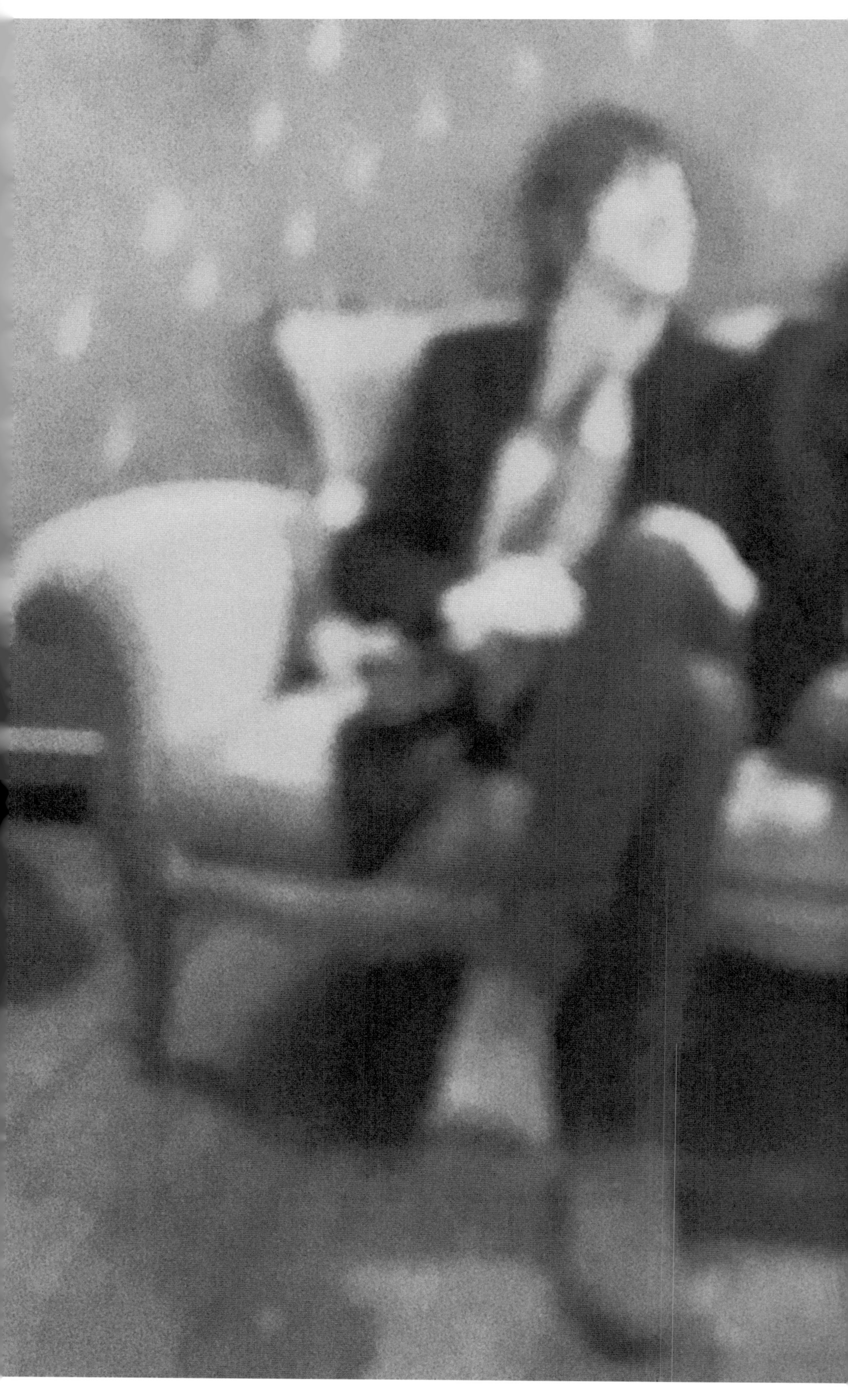

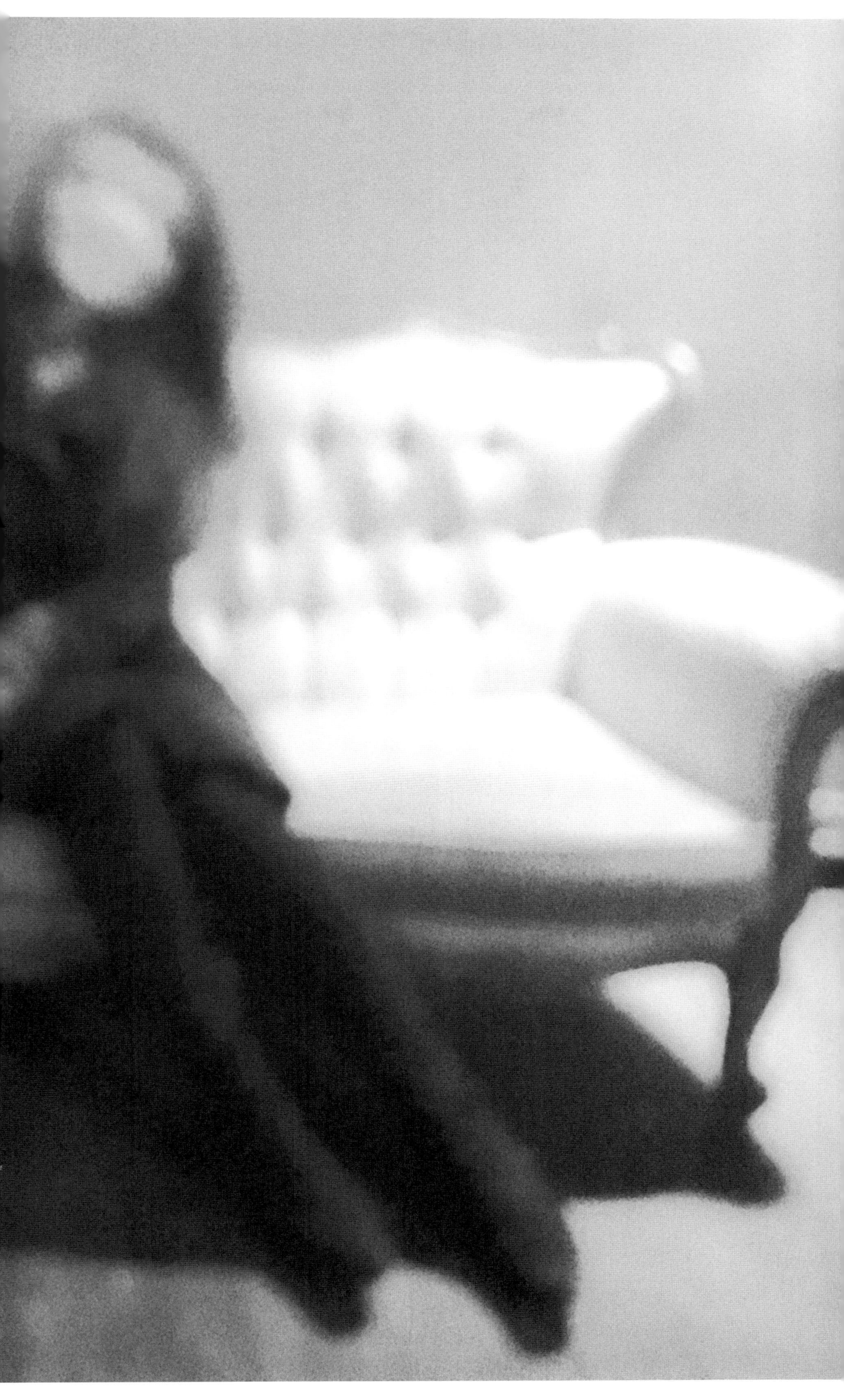

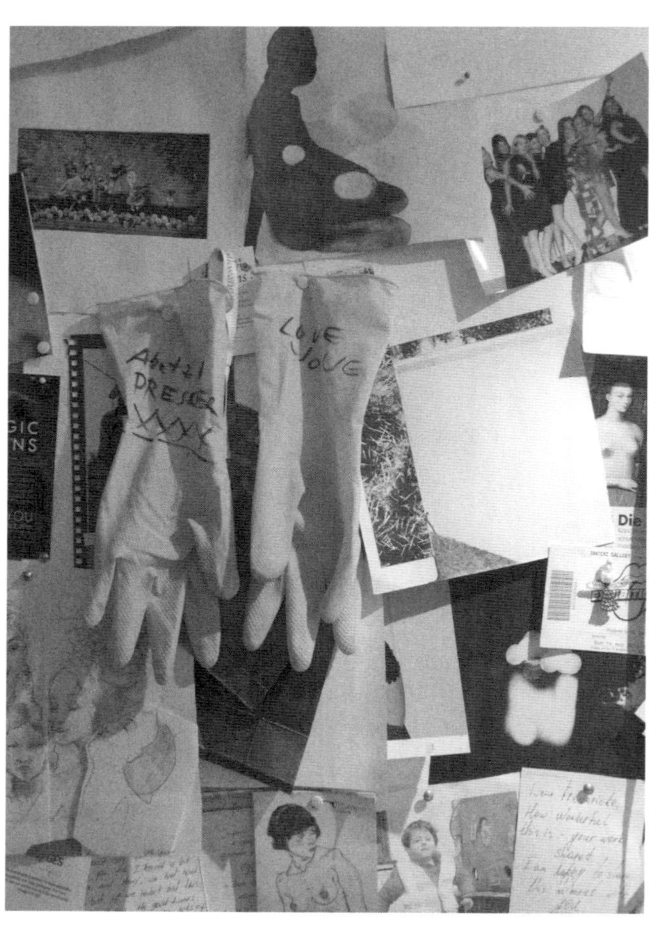

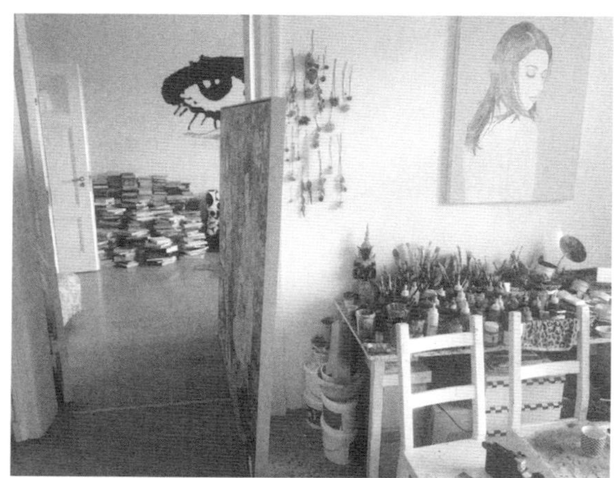

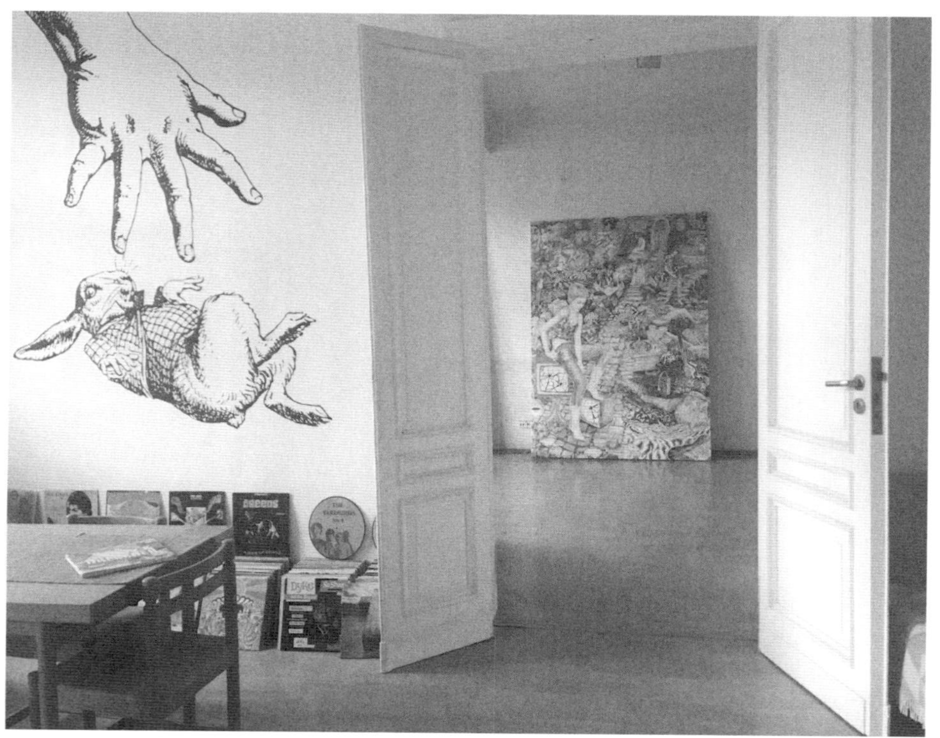

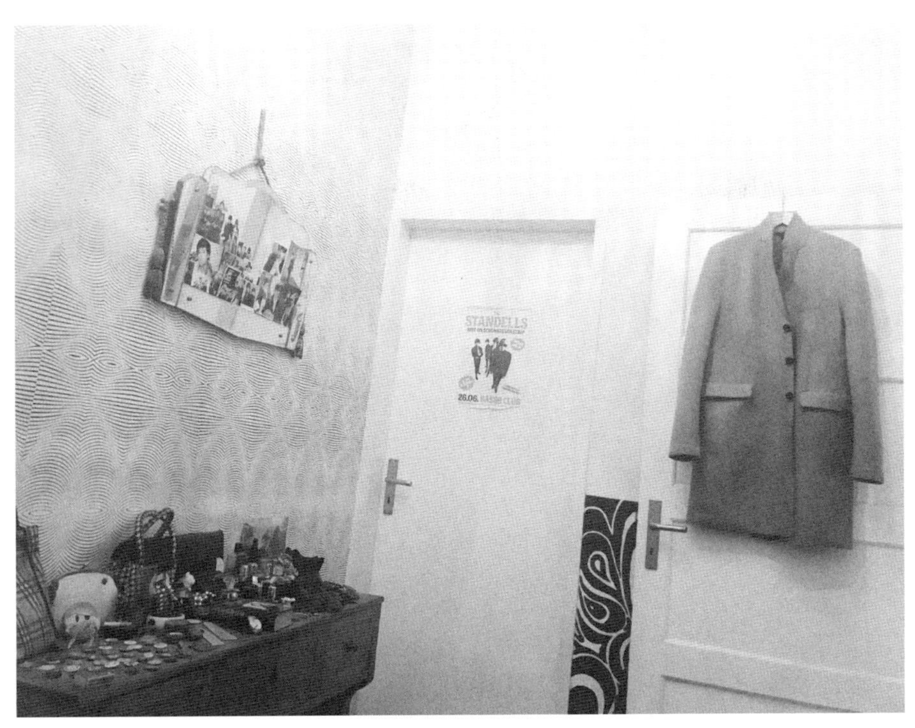
STANDELLS
26.06.

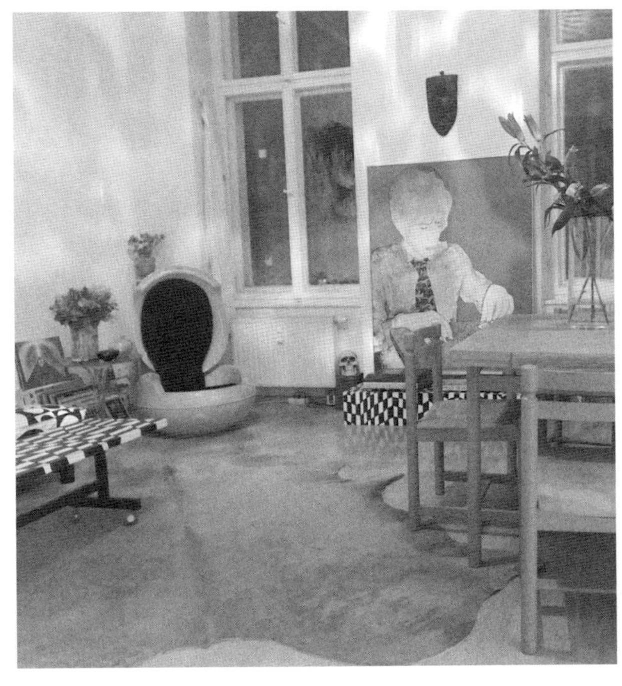

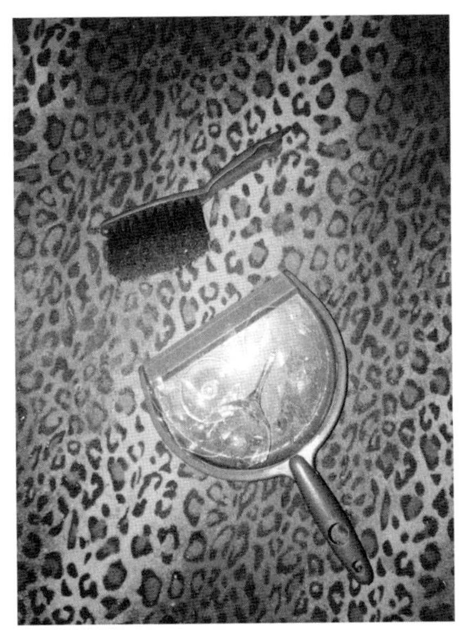

Werkliste / List of Works

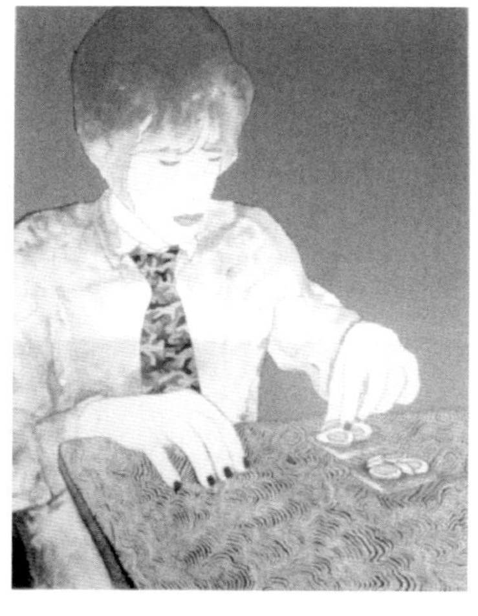

S./p. 2
Up Against It, 1997
Acryl auf Leinwand

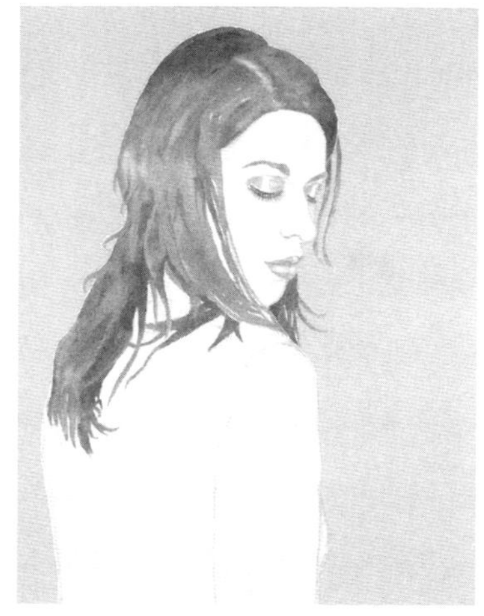

S./p. 3
Atmosphères, 2000
Acryl auf Leinwand

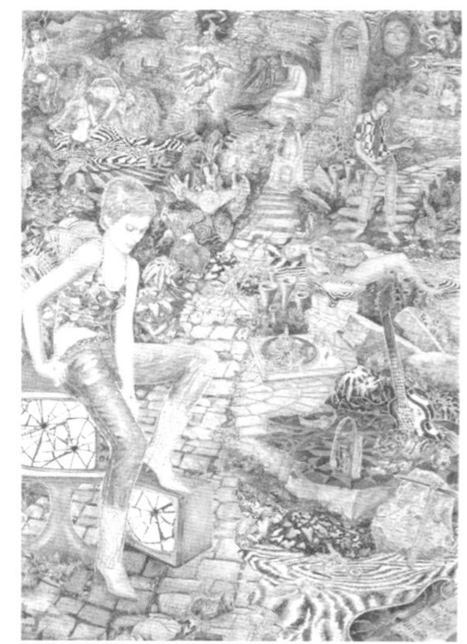

S./p. 5
Yeah Yeah Yeah, 2005
Acryl auf Leinwand

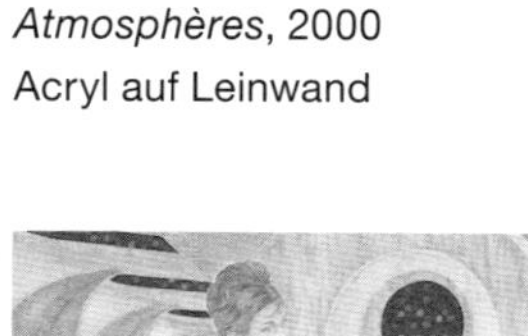

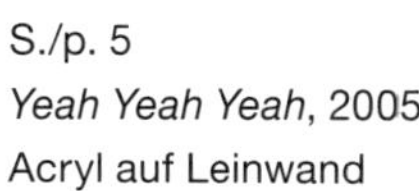

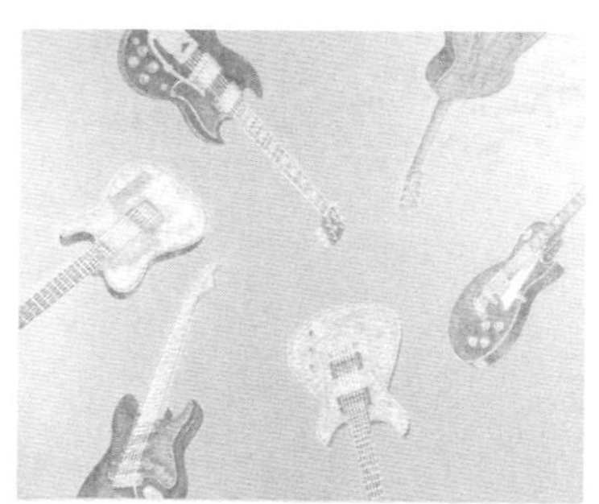

S./p. 6-7
Soul Explosion, 2019
Acryl auf Leinwand

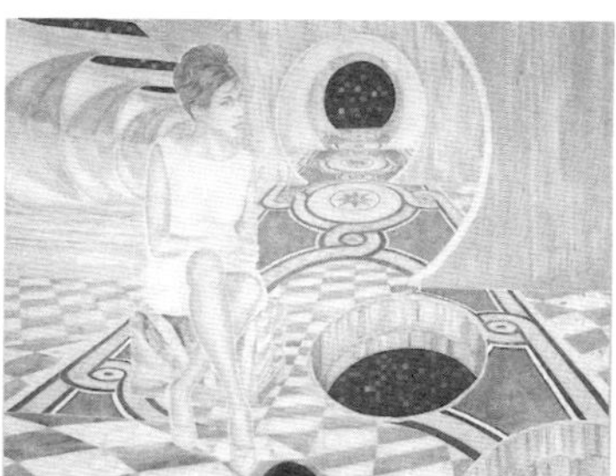

S./p. 8-9
Answer My Prayer, 2018
Acryl auf Leinwand

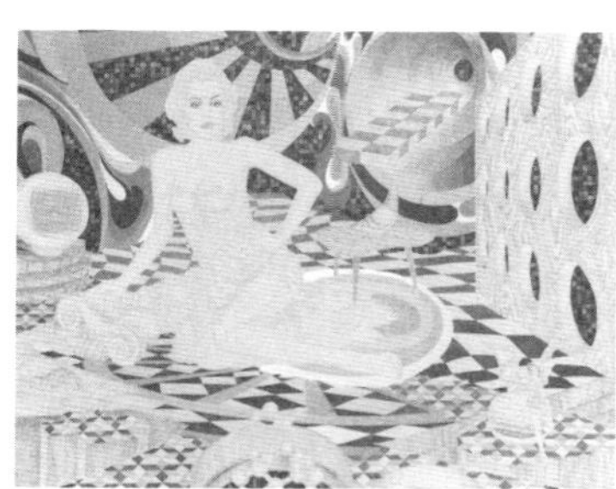

S./p. 10-11
Birthday, 2017
Acryl auf Leinwand

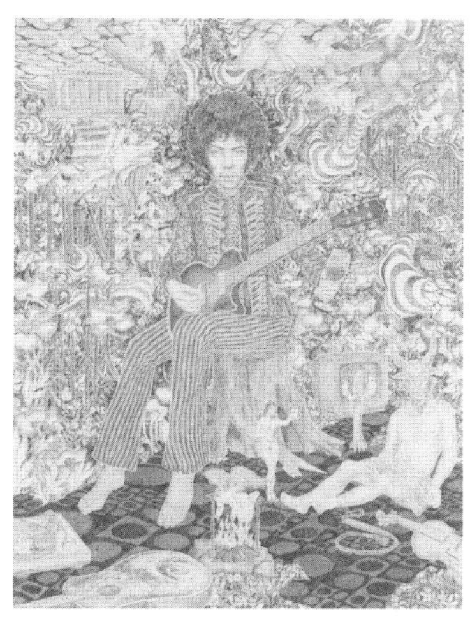

S./p. 12
Room Full of Mirrors, 2011
Acryl auf Leinwand

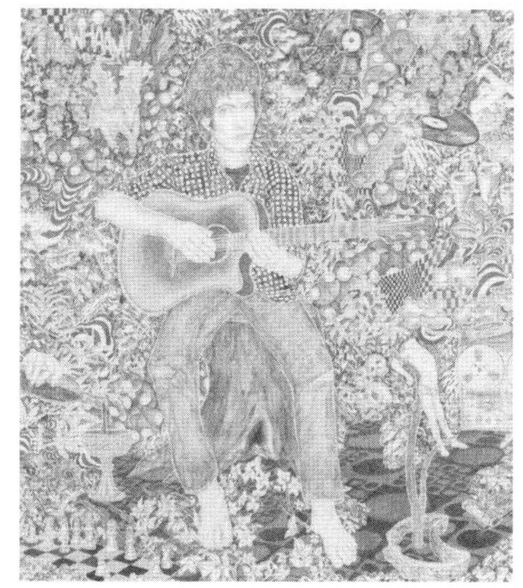

S./p. 13
Bob Dylan, 2011
Acryl auf Leinwand

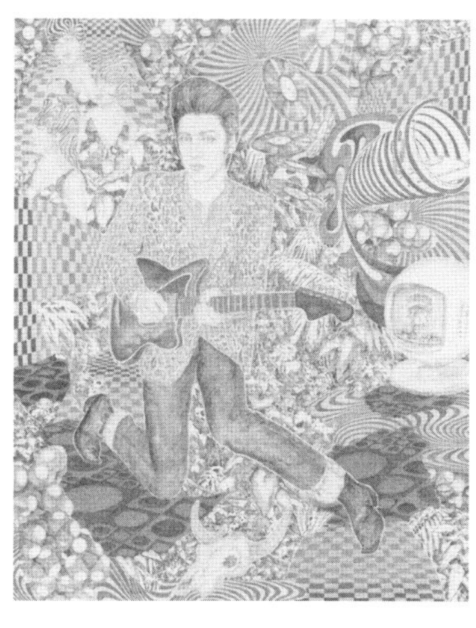

S./p. 15
Elvis Presley, 2011
Acryl auf Leinwand

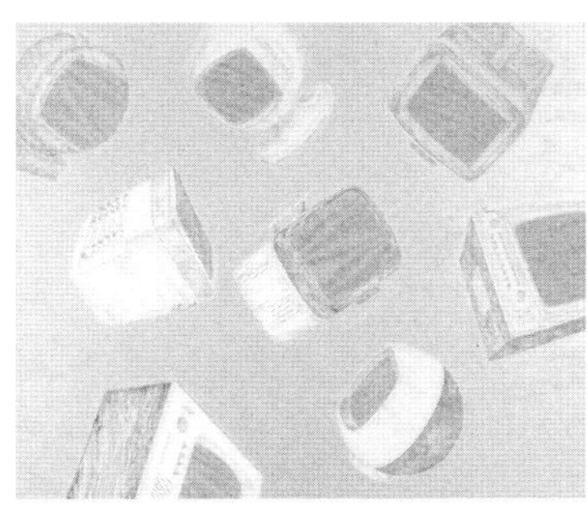

S./p. 16-17
Galaxies, 2019
Acryl auf Leinwand

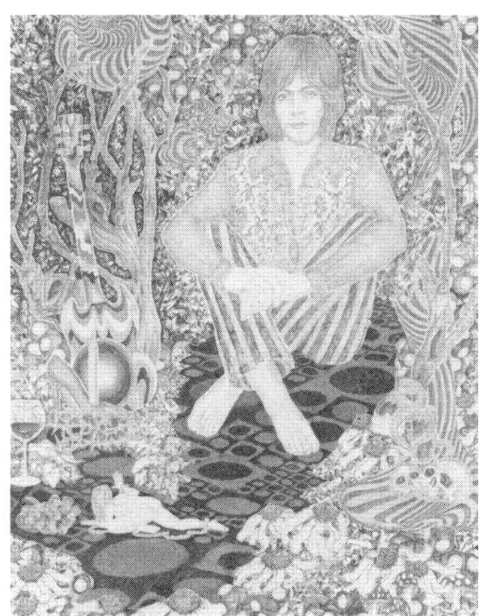

S./p. 18
Eric Clapton, 2011
Acryl auf Leinwand

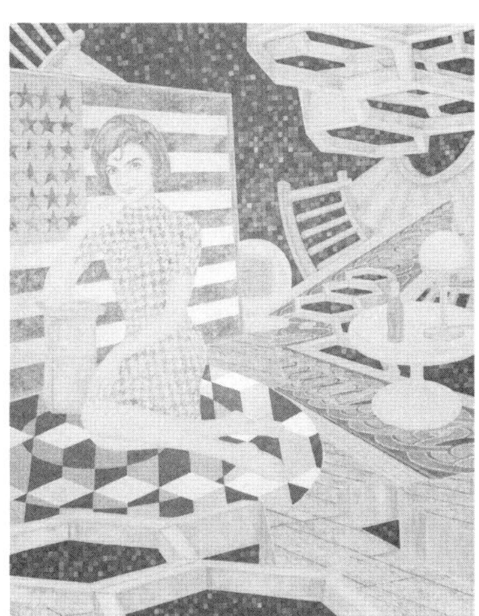

S./p. 19
Rebirth, 2018
Acryl auf Leinwand

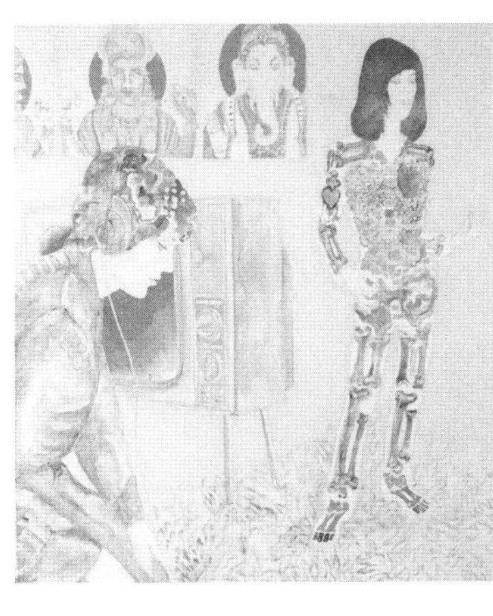

S./p. 21
A Ticket to the World of Unlimited Mobility, 1998
Acryl auf Leinwand

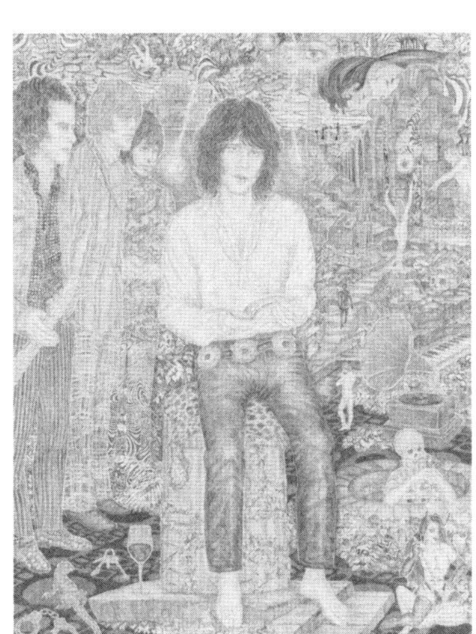

S./p. 64
The Doors, 2011
Acryl auf Leinwand

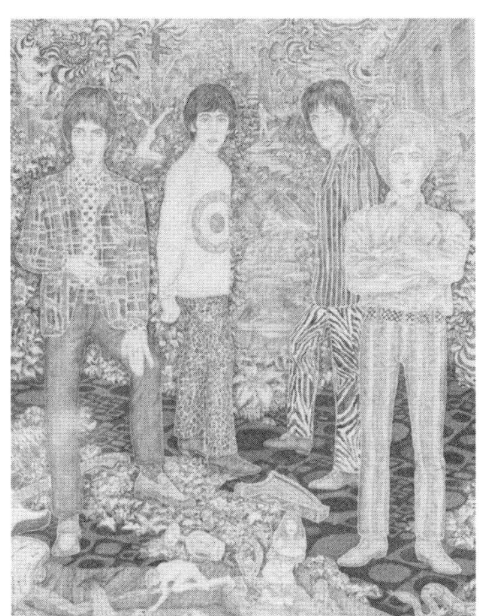

S./p. 65
The Who, 2011
Acryl auf Leinwand

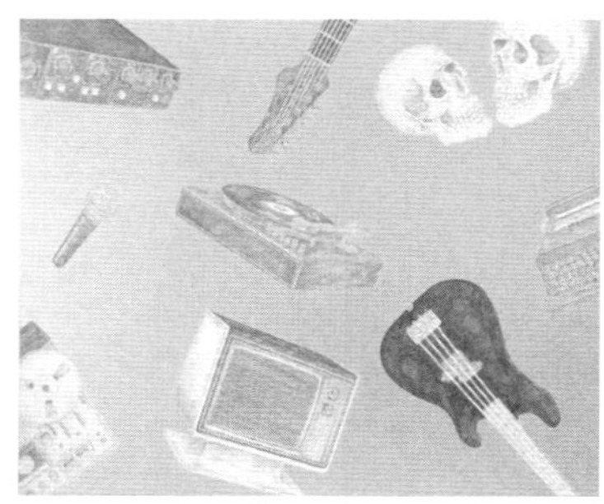

S./p. 66-67
On the Road, 2019
Acryl auf Leinwand

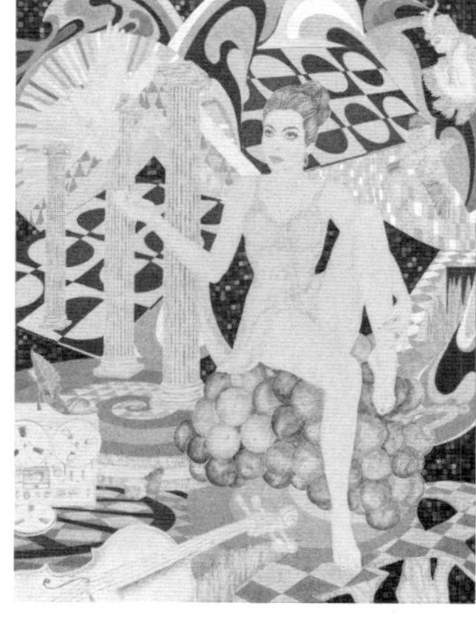

S./p. 68
Maria Callas, 2017
Acryl auf Leinwand

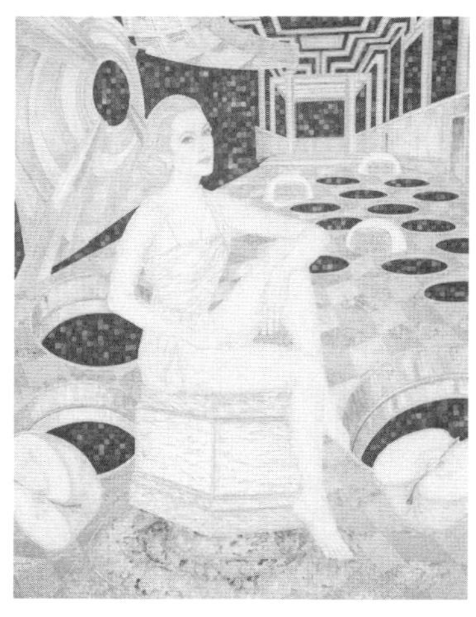

S./p. 69
Flashback, 2018
Acryl auf Leinwand

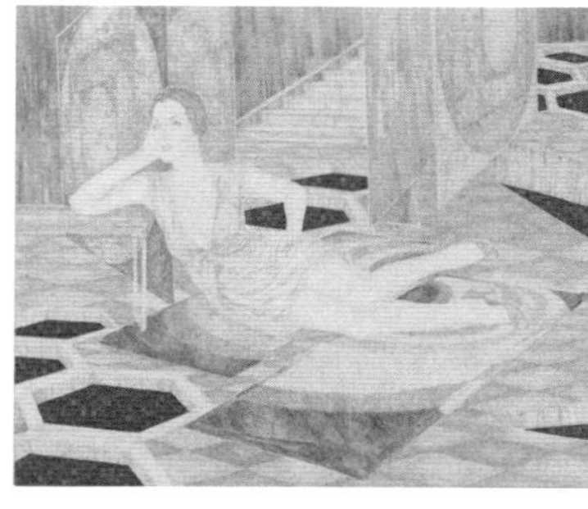

S./p. 70-71
Passage, 2019
Acryl auf Leinwand

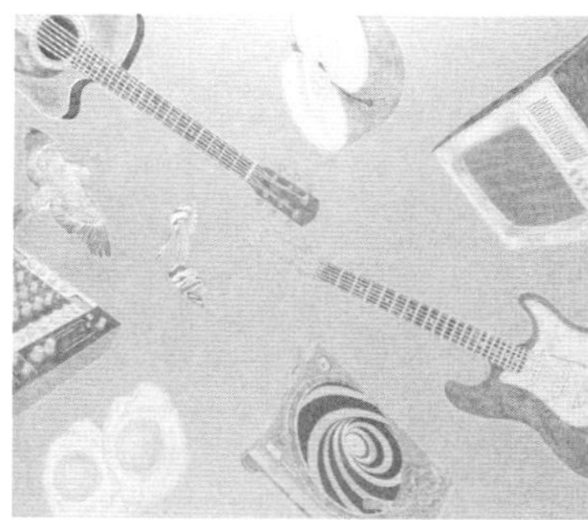

S./p. 72-73
A Place Called Love, 2019
Acryl auf Leinwand

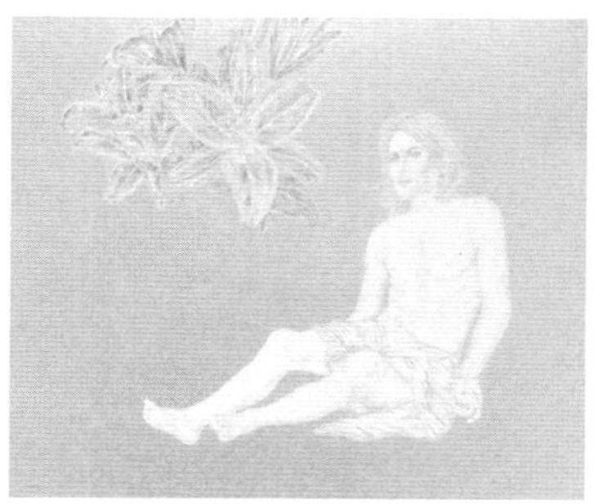

S./p. 74
Resurrection, 2019
Acryl auf Leinwand

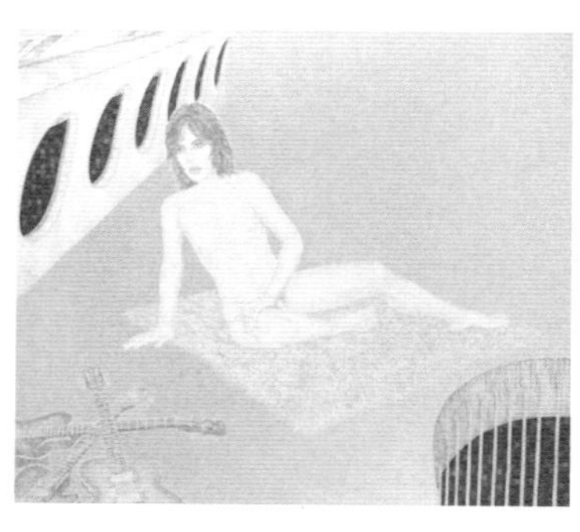

S./p. 75
Intersection, 2019
Acryl auf Leinwand

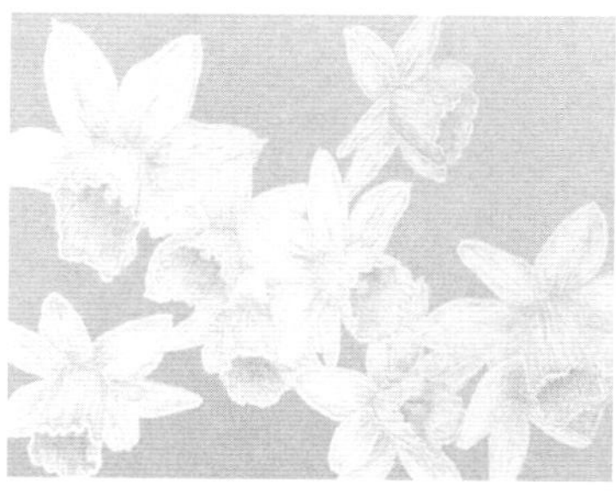

S./p. 76-77
Golden Down, 2019
Acryl auf Leinwand

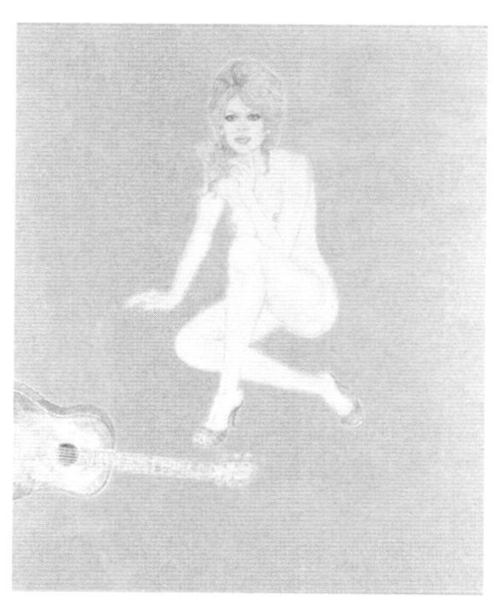

S./p. 78
Backstage, 2019
Acryl auf Leinwand

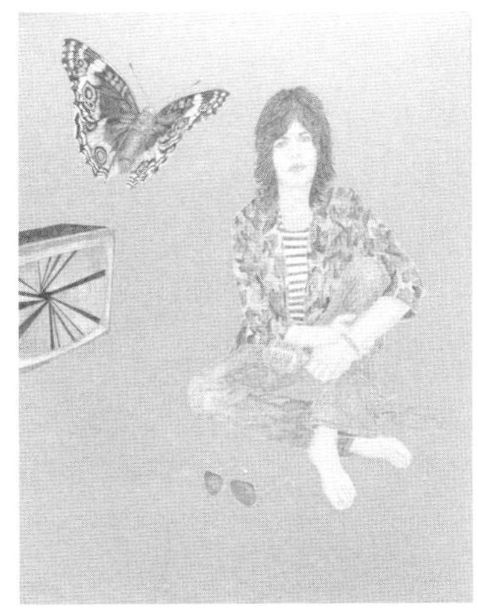

S./p. 79
Sympathy for the Devil, 2019
Acryl auf Leinwand

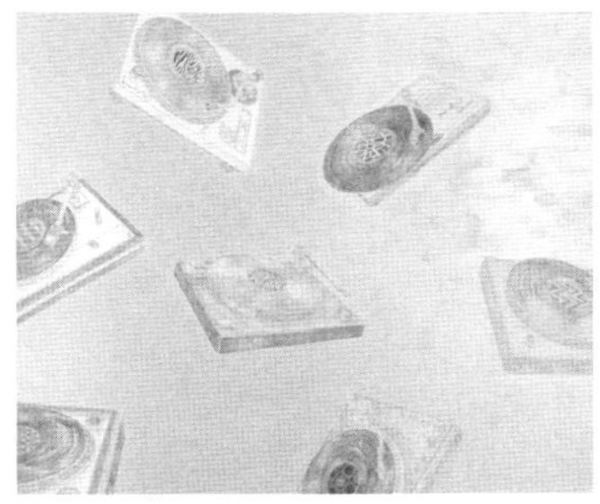

S./p. 80-81
Supernature, 2019
Acryl auf Leinwand

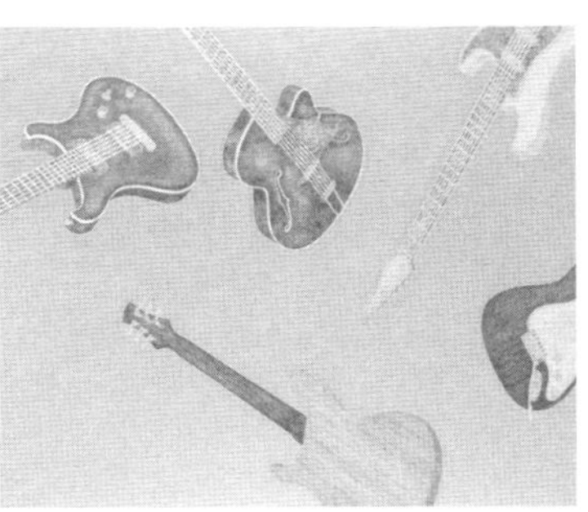

S./p. 82-83
Stardust, 2019
Acryl auf Leinwand

Abetz & Drescher
Place Called Love

This publication was released on the occasion of the exhibition *Place Called Love* by the Berlin-based artist duo Abetz & Drescher, conceived for the Kunsthalle Rostock. It is their first institutional solo exhibition resulting from a period of creative collaboration that has spanned over twenty years.

Maike Abetz and Oliver Drescher met at the Kunstakademie Düsseldorf in 1994, where they both studied under Alfonso Hüppi[1] during different semesters. In 1995, they moved to Berlin together to study with Katharina Sieverding through 1997 at the Hochschule der Künste. They have been working as an artist duo since 1995, creating collaborative works of art under the name Abetz & Drescher. The couple's new beginning in Berlin, which ran parallel to the post-reunification dynamics of the city, was decisive in shaping their painting career, artistic development, and recognizable visual language.
Their paintings embody dreams, illusions, hallucinations, and reflections of society using aspects of mass cultures such as music, art, and science fiction films as examples. The couple creates a symbiosis that encompasses the period from the 1960s to the 1990s and includes icons of international music such as Mick Jagger, Jimi Hendrix, Bob Dylan, Eric Clapton, and The Who. These are immortalized in painterly representations, accompanied by their instruments and sometimes by the artists themselves, who are frequently staged as protagonists of their own narratives.
The result is the reproduction of a dynamic, diverse, lively scenario, immersed in a psychedelic world of mass culture as well as a journey into the past, including themes of the present and future. This suits the ideology and lifestyle of Abetz & Drescher, who regard music as a central figure in their works as well as a guide and reflection of society.

Staging as a Gesamtkunstwerk

The exhibition *Place Called Love* transforms Kunsthalle Rostock's atrium into a Gesamtkunstwerk in which Abetz & Drescher's paintings, created between 1997 and 2019, become part of the whole. The fusion of the utopia seen in the works takes place in a closed space. Visitors re-encounter the collage-like, central elements of painting in space – an inviting, colorfully patterned, psychedelic capsule, inhabited by players of mass culture and their musical inspiration.

The Kunsthalle Rostock's atrium bears witness to its own transformation. The boundaries of the canvases are dissolved, creating a sense of unity within the space. The paintings are the reproduction of a staging – inhabited in a real or imaginary way by elements from the artist's everyday universe. The paintings are complemented by three walls, and the presentation does not conform to conservative hanging but is organized in a dense combination of themes and series. The visualization of this Gesamtkunstwerk becomes more concrete as individual components of the images conquer the space. A disco ball, mirrored floor, colorful carpets, beanbag chairs, and black-and-white wallpaper created by the artists in an Op-Art style are placed throughout the space. In the background, songs that complement the Abetz & Drescher repertoire can be heard.[2]

Different elements from music, design, fashion, architecture, and painting are inserted with a methodical composition. They are components of the painting and are detached from the medium to conquer the exhibition hall. The aesthetic structures of the paintings prove themselves to be part of reality.

The visitors, in turn, assume the role of the painting's protagonists. This backdrop influences their facial expressions, gestures, and postures. As on a stage or in a film set, they act as performers according to a script supplied by the artist duo: looking at the paintings, listening to music, lounging, immersing themselves in the psychedelic landscape. Reality and scenario overlap without a visible border. In this way, one recognizes the true work of art, as Walter Benjamin might explain: “Let us compare the screen on which a film unfolds with the canvas of a painting. The painting invites the spectator to contemplation; before it, the spectator can abandon himself to his associations. Before the movie frame he cannot do so. No sooner has his eye grasped a scene than it is already changed. It cannot be arrested.”[3] The experience in space cannot be fixed under the physical or psychological encounters since the visitors activate this scenery through their presence and perception. To be part of this artistic installation means to awaken memories and associations.

Curiosity and hope are the motivating factors that contribute to artists and viewers meeting in such complex artistic contexts. The dynamic is similar to the consumption of goods. Still, the content and result of an intensive cultural encounter do not enrich the ego like trivially consumed goods: “The consumption of art and products of other creative activities – literature, philosophy, science, and everything in between – i.e., the consumption of products of other people's creativity, always contains something unexpected, new, surprising, something that transcends concrete existing need. This leads to – however paradoxical this may sound – the satisfaction of the special need for the new, for the expansion of the existing, for the confrontation with the unknown, in short, the need for the inner renewal of the consumer. The consumer does not seek – or does not primarily seek – only confirmation of himself.”[4] It is not only the artist who is a committed consumer of art, but also all those who have not become resigned. *Place Called Love* is a platform designed to sharpen the human senses and perception.

Oeuvre of the Bon Vivant

Maike Abetz and Oliver Drescher live their art, which is a faithful representation of their existence. There are countless artist couples who have seized their place in art history, such as Gilbert and George,[5] Christo and Jeanne-Claude,[6] Eva and Adele,[7] Bernd and Hilla Becher,[8] Elmgreen & Dragset,[9] and Fischli/Weiss,[10] and who – as the result of a symbiosis – conceive and realize their projects only as a couple. And, as Abetz & Drescher do, they also deal with painting, like Römer & Römer.[11] Numerous exhibitions have focused on the theme of the artist couple or artist duo to distinguish whether both artists pursue their own artistic careers or, as with Abetz & Drescher, create collaborative artistic work.[12] This artistic existence raises several questions: " … creative exchange or influence? Rivalry? Self-empowerment of the female partner? Artistic and personal harmony?"[13]

Abetz & Drescher emphasize that when they met, there was a natural interest in common themes and a way of life, as well as the urge to invent something new for themselves as enrichment for both.[14] From the very beginning, Maike Abetz was considerably interested in painting and focused intensively on pictorial characteristics and her role models. She euphorically tells us that the painter Sigmar Polke, who died in 2010, and especially his iconic work *Höhere Wesen: rechte obere Ecke schwarz malen!* (Higher beings commanded: paint the upper right corner black!),[15] which was created exactly fifty years ago, had influenced her artistic practice. The banality of the title, the motif (black triangle on white ground), and even the banal rhyme (command – paint) could be references to spiritual influences, pure irony of the artist, or an effective way to defend an artist's autonomy in the creative process by finding a distraction or excuse to distract the focus from his artistic decision. It was more than Polke's attitude that attracted Abetz' attention, also the way he composed his canvases and pictures in general: "Especially in Sigmar Polke's paintings there are numerous traces of a changing society: trivial scenes, banalities of everyday life, petty bourgeois ambitions, national and international politics – these were the themes he dissected under the magnifying glass of his relentless analysis. He delivered a unique version of reality, interspersed with irony, humor, and criticism. His alchemy combines intuition, planning, and chance, and the material also played its part. Experimental curiosity has always been one of his traits. It was also what drove him to play with all available techniques and genres: painting, drawing, gouache, photography, object art, films, and editions."[16]

Meanwhile, Oliver Drescher's interests are mainly anchored in philosophy: "As philosophers, it is above all the French like Michel Foucault, Roland Barthes, Paul Virilio, Gilles Deleuze who should be mentioned. But the German media theorist Friedrich Kittler is also very important. I also studied with him. Sculptors would be those from the 1960s: Claes Oldenburg, James Rosenquist, Jasper Johns, Tom Wesselmann, George Segal. But also very important: Martin Kippenberger and Mike Kelley."[17] His primary focus is always considering the content, asking questions, and lending structure. At the beginning of his studies, he was interested in sculpture, which for him can transform thoughts into concrete forms.

But the symbiosis between Maike Abetz and Oliver Drescher finally crystallizes in painting. The use of acrylic paint on large canvases reflects the fusion of the two artists – their interest, their way of painting, aesthetic, and content-related arguments are summarized under the signature Abetz & Drescher, without leaving traces of the individual identities for the viewer. Their works correspond to the spirit of the Berlin art scene of the mid-1990s and find significant resonance as a component of new German painting: "At first sight, the painting of Maike Abetz and Oliver Drescher, seems about to explode with colour, to be wallowing in the drastic vividness of a sixties revival, to primarily collect representatives of a pop culture getting a bit too long in the tooth, albeit shown in their prime as in the 'Viva' magazine. But the links go much further, ancient gods and baroque cherubs can also be found alongside arches from ancient Greece which suddenly flow into op-art ornaments. The pictures are time machines, they produce hyper-historical and, simultaneously, syn-aesthetical spaces which, in particular, transform the medium of music into the visual and unite codes to form densely staggered allegories."[18]

The genre of the self-portrait is a significant component of their oeuvre, either individually or integrated into their universe, which is shaped by music. In the style of the 1960s and 1970s, the protagonists are portrayed with the typical ornaments of the time. They are an integral part of their self-portrayal, staging, and perception. Martin Kippenberger was a comrade-in-arms of self-dramatization, who repeatedly critically or ironically portrayed and questioned his own role. His first solo exhibition in 1981 at the nGbK (Neue Gesellschaft für bildende Kunst, Berlin) was titled *Lieber Maler, male mir …* (Dear Painter, paint for me …). It was an ironic reference to the role of the artist and his self-portrayal in painting: "Kippenberger's title *Lieber Maler, male mir …* articulates a radical statement about the contemporary status of the painter. His directive should be taken at face value: 'Dear painter, paint me,' 'Dear painter, paint for me,' or 'Dear painter, paint me something,' Kippenberger is not only making a sarcastic delegation of artistic responsibility but he is clearly confirming that the 'dear' figure of the painter has lost his cultural currency."[19] This critical statement was partly due to the fact that the series of twelve works presented by Martin Kippenberger in the exhibition were the result of a commissioned cinema poster painter. His task was to imitate the artist in the poster motifs in his role as an artist.

In addition to self-portrait, Abetz & Drescher's figurative painting is always inhabited by two central figures: the artist themselves, who may pose for each other, as in the works *Atmosphères* (2000) or *Up Against It* (1997); female muses as divas and pin-up figures; or musicians who provide the inspiration for artistic creation through their songs. The homage is emphasized in the title of the pictures: Maria Callas, Jimi Hendrix, Mick Jagger, The Who, The Doors, Elvis Presley – numerous myths are celebrated with these persons and titles.

The color palette has an authentic relationship to legendary vintage pictures in a combination of orange, red, pink, blue, and silver. The main characters – especially in the "musician series" – are placed in front of a vivid background, the entire surface of which is part of the narrative. Individual scenes mix and the effect of the picture-in-picture hypnotizes the viewer. Attention is drawn to the magical, graphic representation of the myths. The eyes stroll restlessly in a dense, constructed landscape with animals, humans, plants, games, pleasures, and all sorts of excesses of life up to the representation of skulls. These intense, surrealistic compositions are reminiscent of reproductions of hallucinogenic experiments, for example, in the works *Mick Jagger*, *The Doors*, and *Eric Clapton*, all created in 2011.

In current works created from 2017 onwards, female representations are celebrated by being presented as individuals centered in the picture. Their attitudes are sovereign, sublime. Their facial expressions and gestures invite the viewer into a direct dialogue. They are seated in interiors that look like room capsules. These are decorated with optical patterns that achieve the illusion of an in-depth perspective. Rooms such as those in the paintings *Rebirth, Answer My Prayer*, and *Flashback* grant a view of the outside world through various openings. As if in a spaceship, the muse orbits the universe as though it were inviolable for humans.

In the most recent works, the individual elements are now dissolved and extracted. Record players or guitars float in front of silver, monochromatic backgrounds like in *Supernature*, *Soul Explosion*, or *Stardust* (all 2019). Abetz & Drescher remain true to their icons and the traces they've left. They achieve an authentic oeuvre using the example of the bon vivant, who they adore and immortalize in their paintings.

The Myth of Pop Culture

In the 1950s, San Francisco was already the beat generation's stage. The protagonists were poets and writers who, together with visual artists such as Bruce Conner,[19] defended a new aesthetic and programmatic approach with a critical view of social trends. Fifty years ago, the legendary Woodstock Festival took place. Thirty-two bands and solo artists performed in front of an estimated 400,000 visitors. The festival was a commercially uncoordinated event and embodied the longing for Love & Peace in a controversial political, social, and economic era.

In the 1960s, the counterculture was on the international agenda. The artistic movements, led by visual artists, writers, filmmakers, fashion designers, and musicians, defended the right to equality in society, regardless of socio-economic background.

It became a historical landmark of mass movements for protests that remain part of the contemporary socio-political agenda to this day: "The 1960s are often discussed in terms of revolution. Throughout the decade and around the world, a generation of young people took direct action, effecting a series of social and political transformations. Fifty years later, government policies resulting from such interventions render a way of life in the West that could have been unimaginable to all but the surest of sixties visionaries. The aesthetic legacies of the period persist, too, felt most strongly in the world of fashion, where so-called 'bohemian chic' continues to make its mark, conjuring memories of a turbulent yet hopeful period of American history. Intellectuals, philosophers, and poets of the day provided mounting evidence that change across all spectra of society was not only possible, but fundamentally preferable."[21]

The movement of the 1960s shaped and inspired Abetz & Drescher and is still decisive for their artistic development and work today. The realization of their exhibition *Place Called Love* at Kunsthalle Rostock reveals that certain themes, debates, and contexts are still present in the anniversary year of the "Summer of Love." At the same time, it is a fortunate coincidence that Kunsthalle Rostock is also celebrating its fiftieth anniversary in 2019. The GDR's only new museum building was opened in 1969. Through this exhibition, we are thus bringing two different contexts that exist simultaneously into a dialogue – on the one hand, the traces of pop culture that emerged in the West in the 1960s, and on the other, a cultural platform from the former "Eastern Bloc," which to this day continues to play its role as a mediator of socio-cultural contexts.

Tereza de Arruda, Curator

1 Alfonso Hüppi (born 1935 in Freiburg im Breisgau) is a Swiss painter, graphic artist, and sculptor. He lives in Baden-Baden and occasionally in Namibia. Between 1974 and 1999, he was professor for painting at the Kunstakademie Düsseldorf.

2 Among others, classics by Jimi Hendrix (*Voodoo Child*, *All Along the Watchtower*, *Third Stone from the Sun*), The Doors (*Light My Fire*, *Break On Through (To the Other Side)*), The Rolling Stones (*Paint It Black*, *Sympathy for the Devil*), Daft Punk (*Da Funk*), Cream (*White Room*), Aretha Franklin (*Think*, *Respect*), Elvis Presley (*Shake, Rattle and Roll*, *Blue Suede Shoes*), The Seeds (*Pictures and Design*), Bob Dylan (*Subterranean Homesick Blues*), Nirvana (*Smells Like Teen Spirit*), Brigitte Bardot (*Ça pourrait changer*), Barn Owl (*Devotion II*, *The Darkest Night Since 1683*), Acid Jesus (*Jesus*), The Supremes (*I Hear a Symphony*), Curtis Mayfield (*Move On Up*).

3 Walter Benjamin, "The Work of Art in the Age of Mechanical Reproduction," in: *Illuminations*, Frankfurt/Main 1999, p. 231.

4 Jan Kotik, "Kunst, Kitsch und Design," in: Harry Pross (ed.), *Kitsch. Soziale und politische Aspekte einer Geschmacksfrage*, Munich 1985, p. 137.

5 Gilbert Prousch (born 1943 in St. Martin in Thurn, Italy) and George Passmore (born 1942 in Plymouth, Great Britain).

6 Christo Wladimirow Jawaschew (born 1935 in Gabrowo, Bulgaria) and Jeanne-Claude (born 1935 as Jeanne-Claude Denat de Guillebon in Casablanca, French Morocco; died 2009 in New York City, US).

7 The artist couple Eva and Adele replace biographical data with figures on body height, bust, waist, and hip, cf. https://de.wikipedia.org/wiki/Eva_%26_Adele#Biographie, retrieved on November 5, 2019.

8 Bernd Becher (actually Bernhard Becher, born 1931 in Siegen; died 2007 in Rostock) and Hilla Becher (born 1934 as Hilla Wobeser in Potsdam; died 2015 in Düsseldorf).

9 Michael Elmgreen (born 1961 in Copenhagen, Denmark) and Ingar Dragset (born 1969 in Trondheim, Norway).

10 Peter Fischli (born 1952 in Zurich, Switzerland) and David Weiss (born 1946 in Zurich, Switzerland; died 2012 in Zurich, Switzerland).

11 Torsten Römer (born 1968 in Aachen, Germany) and Nina Römer (born 1978 as Nina Tangian in Moscow, Russia).

12 Cf. among others *Künstlerpaare: Liebe, Kunst und Leidenschaft*, Wallraf-Richartz-Museum & Fondation Corboud, Cologne October 31, 2008–February 8, 2009 and Gemeentemuseum, Den Haag February 21–June 1, 2009; Artist Lovers, Liverpool Biennial. September 24, 1999–November 7, 1999.

13 Konstanze Crüwell, "Künstlerpaare: In jedem Fall sind die Partner vernichtet," *Frankfurter Allgemeine Zeitung*, January 6, 2009. https://www.faz.net/aktuell/feuilleton/kunst/kuenstlerpaare-in-jedem-fall-sind-die-partner-vernichtet-1591578.html, retrieved on November 5, 2019.

14 During a conversation in the artist's studio in Berlin on October 17, 2019.

15 *Höhere Wesen: rechte obere Ecke schwarz malen!,* 1969, synthetic paint on canvas, 151.2 x 126.1 x 3 cm, 165 x 139 x 11 cm (with frame), The Van Abbemuseum Collection, purchased 1977, inventory number 767.

16 Tereza de Arruda, *Sigmar Polke: The Editions*, me Collectors room Berlin / Stiftung Olbricht, Cologne 2017, p. 34.

17 During a conversation in the artist's studio in Berlin on October 17, 2019.

18 Christoph Tannert, *New German Painting*, Munich, Berlin, London, New York 2007, p. 67.

19 Alison M. Gingeras, "Lieber Maler, male mir ..." in: *"Dear Painter, paint me ...". Painting the Figure since late Picabia*, exh. cat., Centre Pompidou, Paris; Kunsthalle Wien, Vienna; Schirn Kunsthalle, Frankfurt/Main 2002, p. 9.

20 Bruce Conner (born 1933 in McPherson, Kansas, US; died 2008 in San Francisco, US).

21 Jill D'Alessandro, Colleen Terry, "What are we fighting for," in: *The Summer of Love. Art, Fashion, and Rock and Roll*, exh. cat, Fine Arts Museums of San Francisco, University of California Press, Berkeley 2017, p. 271.

Interview Tereza de Arruda and Abetz & Drescher

T.A.: You first met in 1994 at the Kunstakademie Düsseldorf. This decision influences your entire existence – when did you decide to work, or to exist as it were, as an artist duo? Was it the themes or the way you painted your works that led to it?

A&D: We met at a party at the Kunstakademie Düsseldorf on December 7, 1994. We've been a couple since then. The collaboration developed out of our desire to bring into art what we both missed in art at the time. When we met, Oliver studied sculpture and Maike painting.
We wanted to overcome the painting of the 1980s and develop a concept for a new kind of painting. For us, not everything had been painted yet; on the contrary, we realized that nothing had been painted yet.

T.A.: Pop culture plays an important role in your artistic representations – be it music, fashion, or design. Is your engagement with these elements about content or aesthetic components?

A&D: We wanted to break down the boundaries between painting, fashion, music, design, media, architecture, philosophy, and (geo)politics. Our paintings are images on images on images. Art means to place. It is a magical act. We were concerned with the formation of identity under media-technical conditions and with storage and transmission.

T.A.: Your images carry a clear, subjective, figurative narrative. The representations and attitudes of the female and male protagonists in the works are simulations of their universe. How important is it for you to stage your own image and existence? What role does the theme of gender theme play in this context?

A&D: The theme of gender and the breaking down of gender stereotypes were very important to us. Judith Butler, who was the initiator of gender theory, should be mentioned here. Judith Butler is influenced by Michel Foucault and Jacques Lacan, who was involved in Surrealist circles. We wanted to dissolve authorship.

T.A.: Man is usually the product of his personal and social relationships. Your works are the product of your personal and social relationships. Without personal and social relationships, man tends to lose his authentic humanity. How can you explain your works as the embodiment of this personal symbiosis?

A&D: We were interested in creating artificial identities. Acquiring, processing, and passing on information. To create images demands the translation of what is subjectively seen into the intersubjective, to dive into a collective field of relation. We wanted to make pop culture and rock'n'roll into protagonists of art.

T.A.: Martin Kippenberger's first solo exhibition in 1981 at nGbK (Neue Gesellschaft für bildende Kunst, Berlin) was called *Lieber Maler, male mir …* (Dear Painter, paint for me …). It was an ironic reference to the role of the artist/painter. What does self-portrayal mean to you in your painting?

A&D: One tendency of art is the elimination of the difference between life and art. We're interested in this suspension – for us, there is no high or low culture. Thus, art creates relationships that lead to authentic humanity. We are protagonists of our own imagery. In our work, we reflect the path from the Ancient Greeks to the Renaissance, from Romanticism to the 1920s all the way to the 60s.

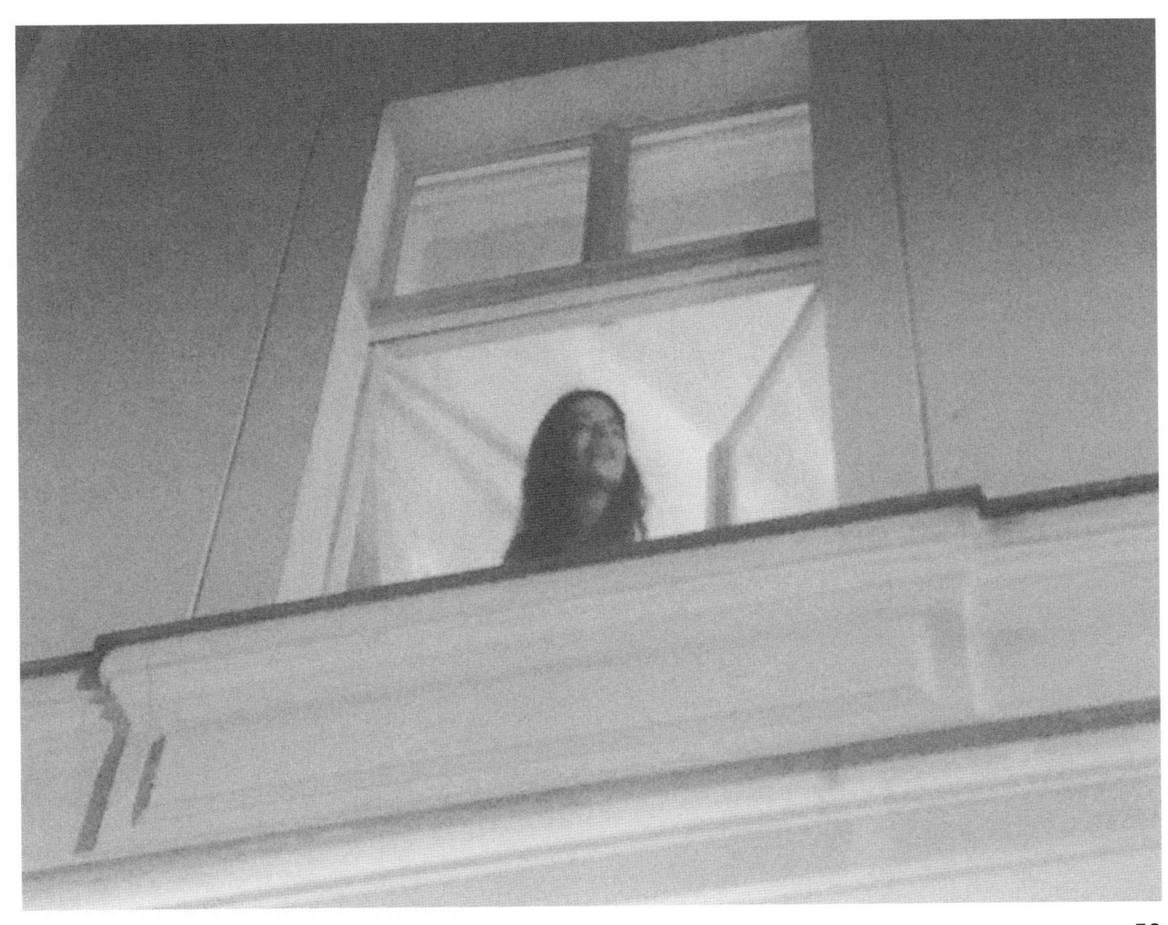

Biografie / Biography

Maike Abetz

Born 1970 in Düsseldorf, DE

Education

1991–1994 Kunstakademie Düsseldorf (with Prof. Alonso Hüppi)

1995–1997 Hochschule der Künste Berlin (with Prof. Katharina Sieverding)

Oliver Drescher

Born 1969 in Essen, DE

Education

1990–1993 Audited lectures with Friedrich Kittler and Vilém Flusser, Ruhruniversität Bochum

1994–1995 Kunstakademie Düsseldorf (with Prof. Alonso Hüppi)

1995–1997 Hochschule der Künste Berlin (with Prof. Katharina Sieverding)

Maike Abetz and Oliver Drescher work since 1995 together and live in Berlin

SOLO EXHIBITIONS

2019 *PLACE CALLED LOVE,* Kunsthalle Rostock, curated by Tereza de Arruda, Rostock, DE
2017 *Dawn of Tomorrow*, Magic Beans, Berlin, DE
2013 *Recent Works*, Galerie Burkhard Eikelmann, Düsseldorf, DE
2012 *Big Bang*, Egbert Baqué Contemporary Art, Berlin, DE
Forever Young, Galerie Suzanne Tarasiève, Paris, FR
2008 *The Modern World Starts Now*, Galerie Suzanne Tarasiève, Paris, FR
2007 *Brave New World*, Goff + Rosenthal, Berlin, DE
2005 Goff + Rosenthal, New York, US
2004 *Paint It Black*, Galerie Suzanne Tarasiève, Paris, FR
2003 *Paint It Black*, Galerie Volker Diehl, Berlin, DE
2000 *Electric Ladyland*, Ars Futura, Zurich, CH
1999 *Close Encounters*, Statements – Art Basel, CFA Berlin, DE
1998 *BOING BUM TSCHAK*, Marc Foxx, Los Angeles, US
1997 *UP AGAINST IT,* Contemporary Fine Arts, Berlin, DE
Fanzine Presentation, Pavillon der Volksbühne, Jugend Musik Festspiele, Berlin, DE

GROUP EXHIBITIONS

2017 *magic+love x art,* curated by Larissa Kikol, Magic Beans, Berlin, DE
2016 *Made in Germany: Contemporary Art from the Rubell Family Collection* at the McNay Art, Museum in San Antonio, Texas, US
Flower Power, Magic Beans, Berlin, DE
2015 *A Rock 'n' Roll Cathedral*, Egbert Baqué Contemporary Art, Berlin, DE
MISAPPROPRIATIONS: New Acquisitions, OCMA – Orange County Museum of Art, Newport Beach, CA, US
2014 *There's a Bluebird in My Heart,* Egbert Baqué Contemporary Art, Berlin, DE
ABRACADABRA, Egbert Baqué Contemporary Art, Berlin, DE
2013 *To Russia with Love and to Lou Reed*, Egbert Baqué Contemporary Art, Berlin, DE
Hauptstrasse – A Tribute to David Bowie, Egbert Baqué Contemporary Art, Berlin, DE
2012 *The Journey to St. Petersburg, Benefit Exhibition for Pussy Riot*, Egbert Baqué Contemporary Art, Berlin, DE
Ten Masterpieces, Galerie Burkhard Eikelmann, Düsseldorf, DE
2011 *Echoes*, Centre Culturel Suisse, Paris, FR
2010 *Portraits de Collectionneurs – Jocelyne et Fabrice Petignat*, Muro Gallery, Geneva, CH
2009 *Flower Power,* CRAA – Centro di Ricerca Arte Attuale, Villa Giulia, IT
BOB – A Tribute to Bob Dylan, Egbert Baqué Contemporary Art, Berlin, DE
With You I Want to Live: Gordon Locksley Collection, Fort Lauderdale Museum of Art, Fort Lauderdale, US

2008 *Sammlung Jocelyne & Fabrice Petignat*, Centre PasquArt, Biel, CH
Gegen den Strich, Bielefelder Kunstverein, Bielefeld, DE
2006 *iPod killed the Video Star*, MAMA Showroom for Media and Moving Art, Rotterdam, NL
The Youth of Today, Schirn Kunsthalle, Frankfurt/Main, DE
2004 Perry Rubinstein Gallery, New York, US
2002 *Televisions*, Kunsthalle Wien, AT
Air Guitar: Art Reconsidering Rock Music, The Cornerhouse, Manchester, UK
Go Johnny Go, Die E-Gitarre – Kunst und Mythos, Kunsthalle Wien, AT
The Ars Futura Show, Ars Futura, Zurich, CH
1999 *Scorpio Rising*, Contemporary Fine Arts, Berlin, DE
Gallery Swap, Sadie Coles HQ, London, UK
D A C H, Galerie Krinzinger, Benger Park, Bregenz, AT
Kraftwerk Berlin, Aarhus Kunstmuseum, Aarhus, DK
Mozart on the Television, New Paintings from Germany, Deitch Projects, New York, US
1998 *View 4*, Mary Boone Gallery, New York, US

ABETZ & DRESCHER BIBLIOGRAPHY

2015 Harald Fricke/Peter Funken, *Rock'n'Roll Cathedral*, Abetz & Drescher
2013 Egbert Baqué, *Hauptstrasse – A Tribute to David Bowie*, Egbert Baqué Contemporary Art, Berlin
2008 Mark Gisbourne, *Künstlerpaare / Double Act: Two Artists, One Expression*, Prestel, Munich
Mark Gisbourne, *Sirens of the Future-Past*, in: *Abetz & Drescher, The Modern World Starts Now*, Suzanne Tarasiève, Paris
2007 *The Upset*, Young Contemporary Painting, Gestalten, Berlin
Christoph Tannert, Justin Hoffmann a. o. (eds.), *Gegen den Strich*, Künstlerhaus Bethanien, Berlin
2006 Christoph Tannert, Jens Asthoff a. o. (eds.), *New German Painting / Neue Deutsche Malerei*, Prestel, Munich
Max Hollein, Matthias Ulrich (eds.), *Youth of Today / Jugend von Heute*, exh. cat. Schirn Kunsthalle, Frankfurt/Main
2004 Christian Ehrentraut, Mark Gisbourne, Abetz & Drescher,
Paint It Black, Galerie Volker Diehl, Berlin; Galerie Suzanne Tarasiève, Paris
2003 Gerald Matt a. o., *GO JOHNNY GO: Die E-Gitarre – Kunst und Mythos*, exh. cat. Kunsthalle Wien, Steidl, Göttingen
2002 Emma Mahony a. o. (eds.), *Air Guitar: Art Reconsidering Rock Music*, Milton Keynes Gallery, Manchester
2001 Gabriele Mackert a. o. (eds.), *Televisions – Kunst sieht fern*, exh. cat. Kunsthalle Wien, Vienna
1999 Anna Elisabeth Kracht, *D A C H*, Galerie Krinzinger, Vienna
Heike Föll, in: *Kraftwerk Berlin*, exh. cat. Aarhus Kunstmuseum, Aarhus

Impressum / Colophon

Dieser Katalog erscheint anlässlich der Ausstellung PLACE CALLED LOVE,
in der Kunsthalle Rostock, 03. November 2019 – 5. Januar 2020

This catalog is published on the occasion of the exhibition PLACE CALLED LOVE,
at Kunsthalle Rostock, November 3rd, 2019 to January 5th, 2020

Herausgeber / Editor
Kunsthalle Rostock

Gestaltung / Design, Produktion / Production Management
Huelsenberg Studio mit Niklas Sagebiel

Text
Tereza de Arruda

Übersetzung / Translation
Alicia Reuter

Lektorat / Copy Editing
DISTANZ Verlag

Fotonachweis / Photo Credits
Marcus Schneider, alle Werke / all paintings
außer / except
Bernd Borchardt, S. / p. 6–9, 16–17, 23, 24, 61–63, 66–67, 72–84
Christian Efremidis, S. / p. 28–29, 38–41
Archiv der Künstler, S. / p. 25–27, 35, 53, 58–60

Lithografie / Image Editing
bildpunkt, Berlin

Gesamtherstellung / Printing and Binding
DZA Druckerei zu Altenburg GmbH

Vertrieb / Distribution
edel Germany GmbH
www.edel.com
international-books@edel.com

ISBN 978-3-95476-313-9
Printed in Germany

Erschienen im / Published by
DISTANZ Verlag
www.distanz.de

Kunsthalle Rostock   EFREMIDIS GALLERY

Ausstellung / Exhibition
Kunsthalle Rostock

Kuratorin / Curator
Tereza de Arruda

Geschäftsführung / Managing Director
Dr. Uwe Neumann

Ausstellungsorganisation und -realisierung / Exhibition Organization and Realization
Heike Heilmann, Christof Kraft, Melanie Ohst

Presse / Press
Fritz Beise

Veranstaltungen / Events
Guntram Porath

Technische Umsetzung / Technical Implementation
Enrico Golly, Christian Meier, Enrico Schwarzer, Claudia Triltsch

Kunsthalle Rostock
Hamburger Str. 40
D-18069 Rostock
T.: +49 381 / 3817000
kunsthalle@rostock.de
www.kunsthallerostock.de

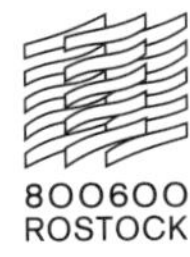

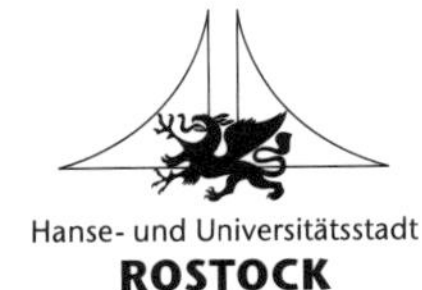

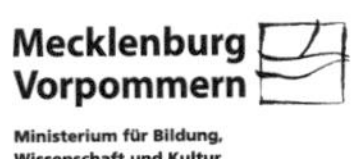

…e result of eight to nine weeks' growth—long, straggly hair at the nape

Side hair forward of the ears is very full in this style, but is not untidy. Careful trimming with scissors achieves correct effect. John Anthony allows little use of electric cutters for lining-out on neck lines and round ears in his salons. He prefers the more natural line produced by scissors

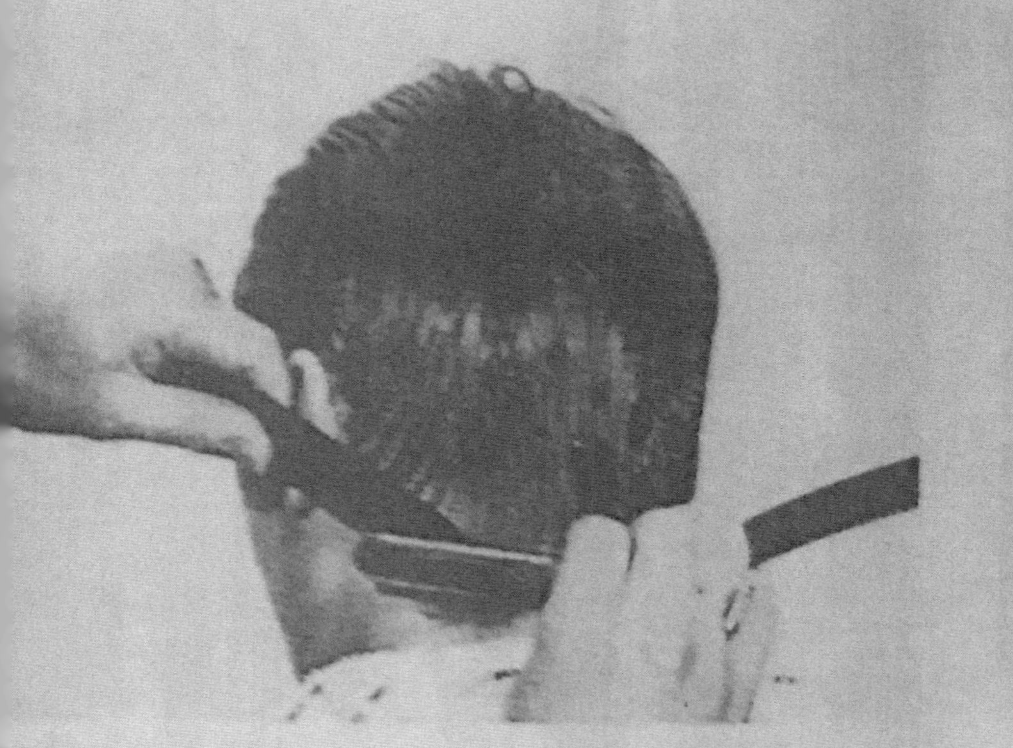

…After shampooing, hair at the nape is razor-cut right down to the ends. …Nape line is cut with the scissors after shampoo, but before razoring. …There is little nape tapering. Hair is lifted on the crown and blended in, but not down to the nape

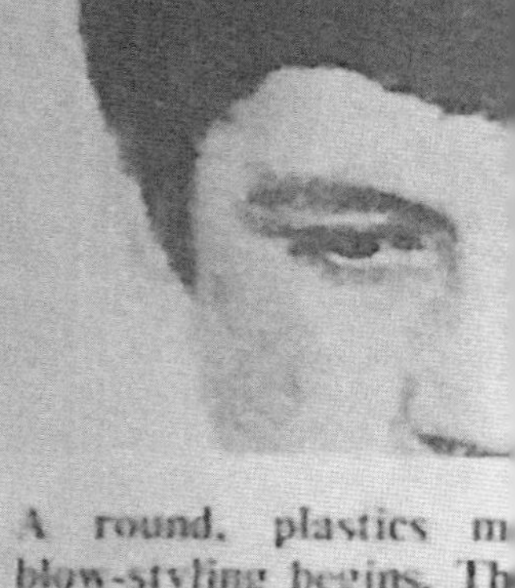

A round, plastics m… blow-styling begins. Th… the hair to be maintai…

Wir bilden uns nicht mehr …ein, dass die mentalen Vorgänge (etwa Wahrneh…nungen, Vorstellungen, Empfindungen, Wünsche, …Gedanken oder Entscheidungen) irgendwelche …inheiten sind, sondern eher, das

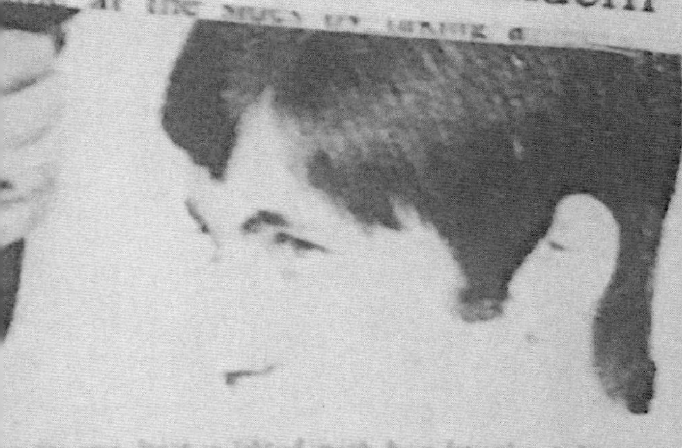

Herstellen künstlicher Gegenstän
künstlicher Materie, künstlicher Lebewes
künstlicher Intelligenzen, künstlicher Identitä
künstlicher Kulturen.

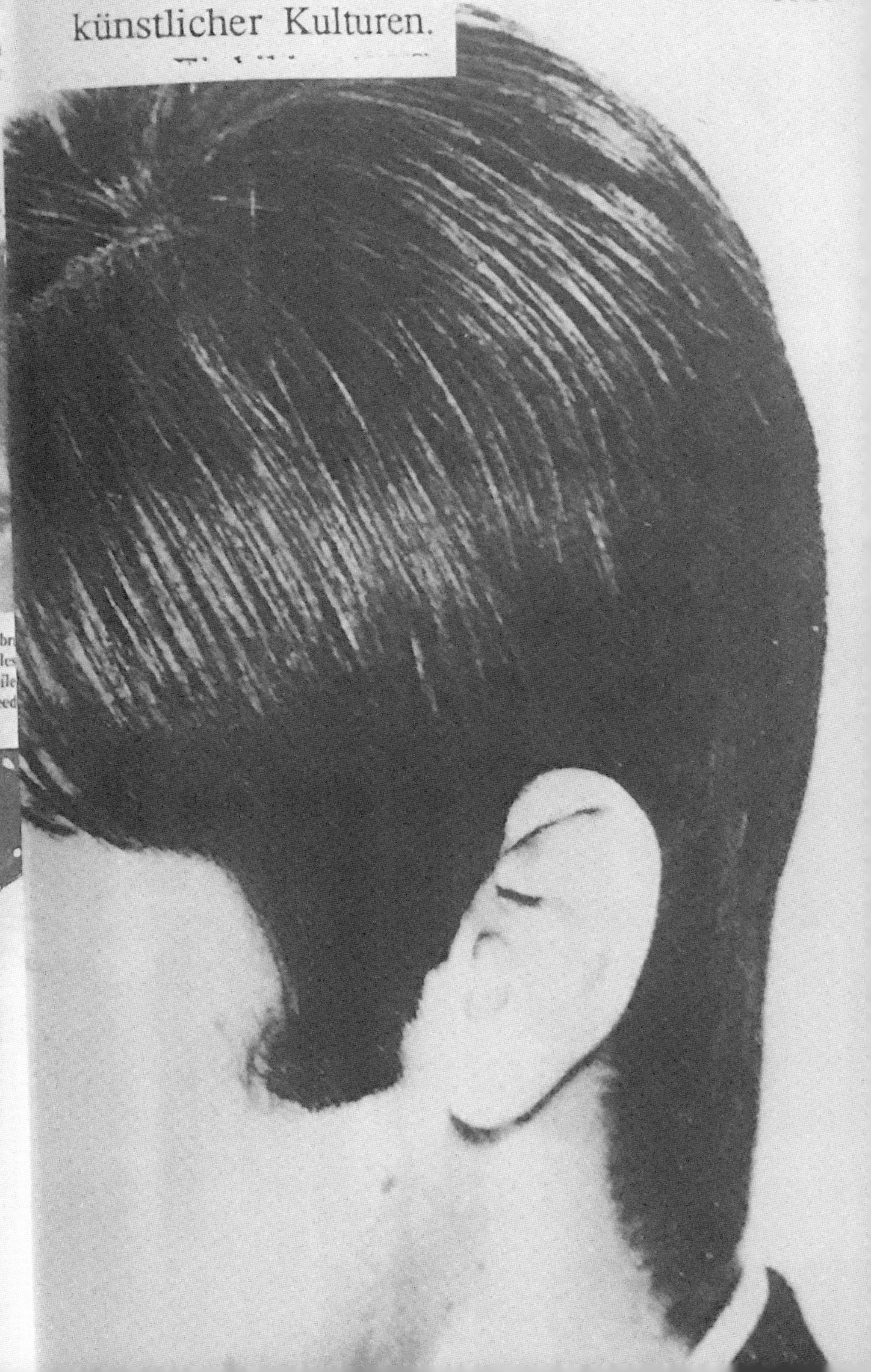

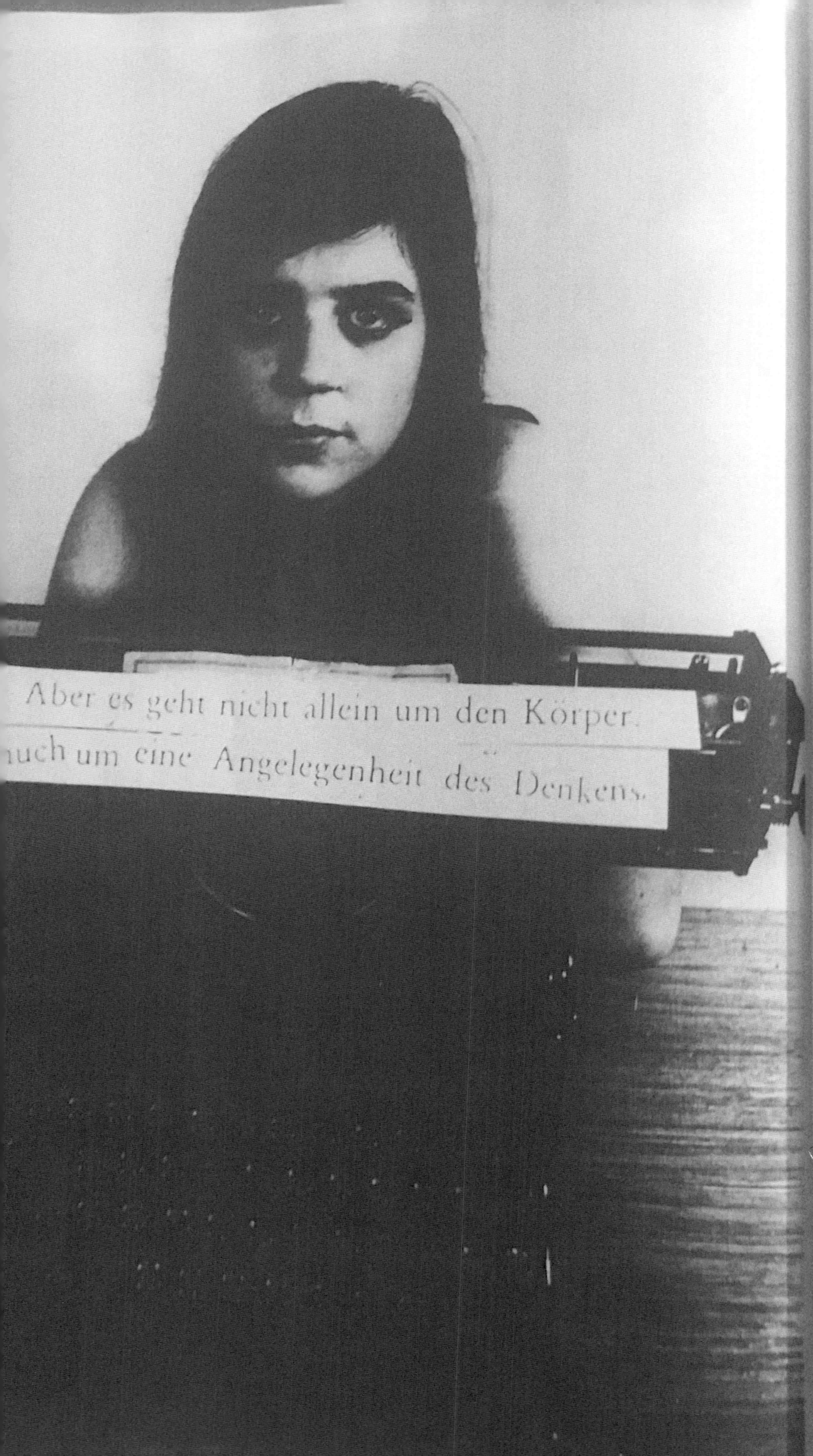
Aber es geht nicht allein um den Körper.
uch um eine Angelegenheit des Denkens.

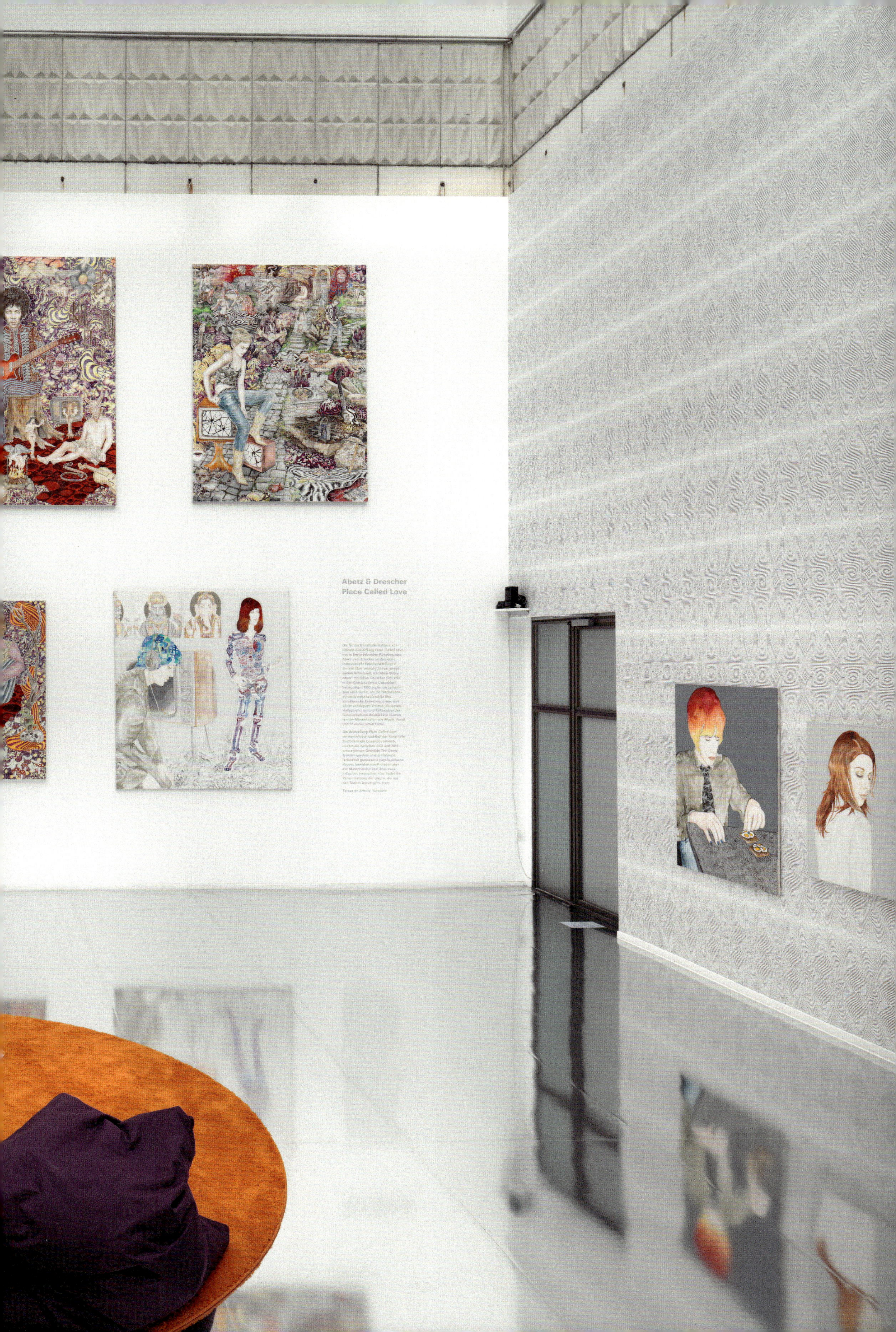
Abetz & Drescher
Place Called Love

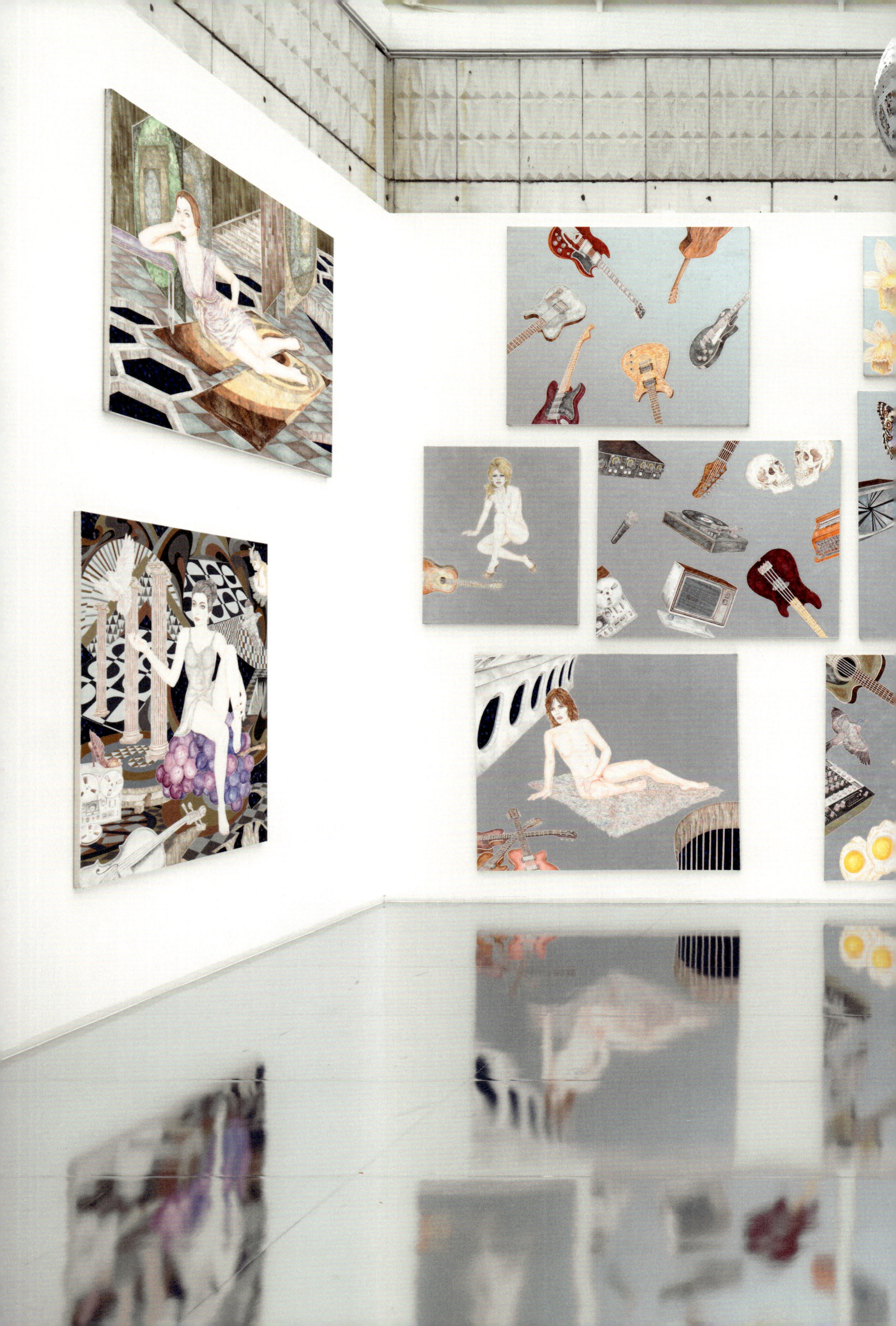

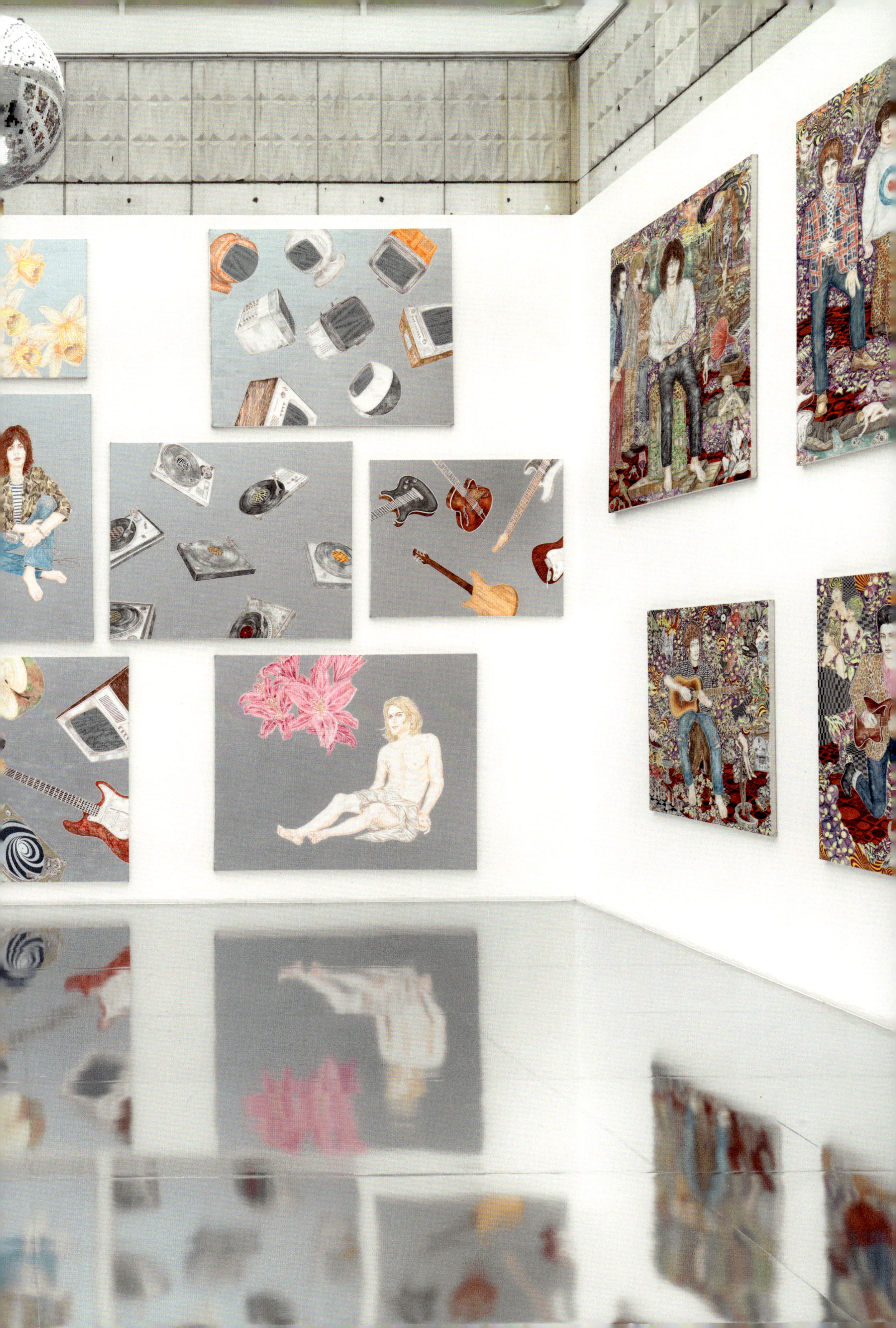

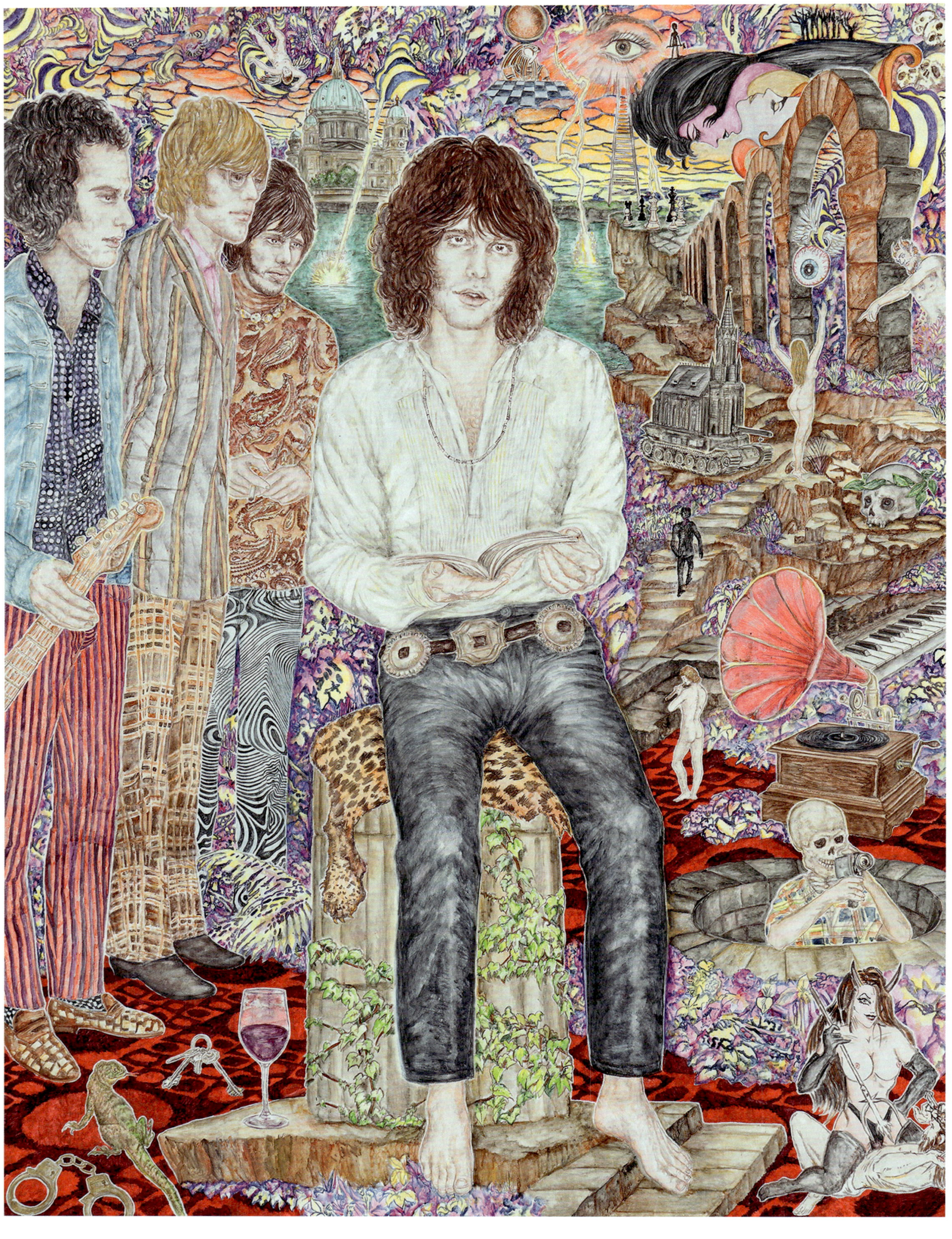

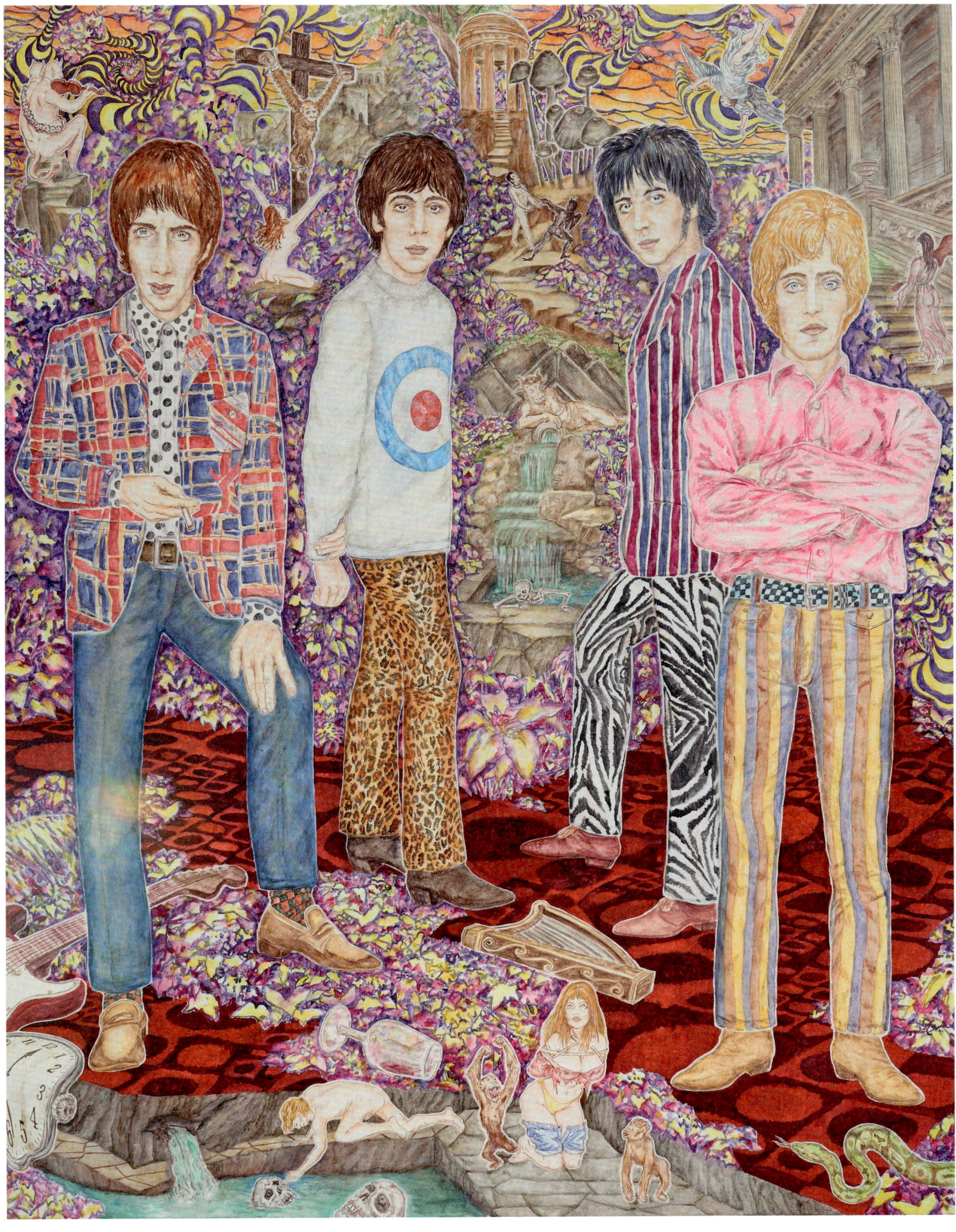

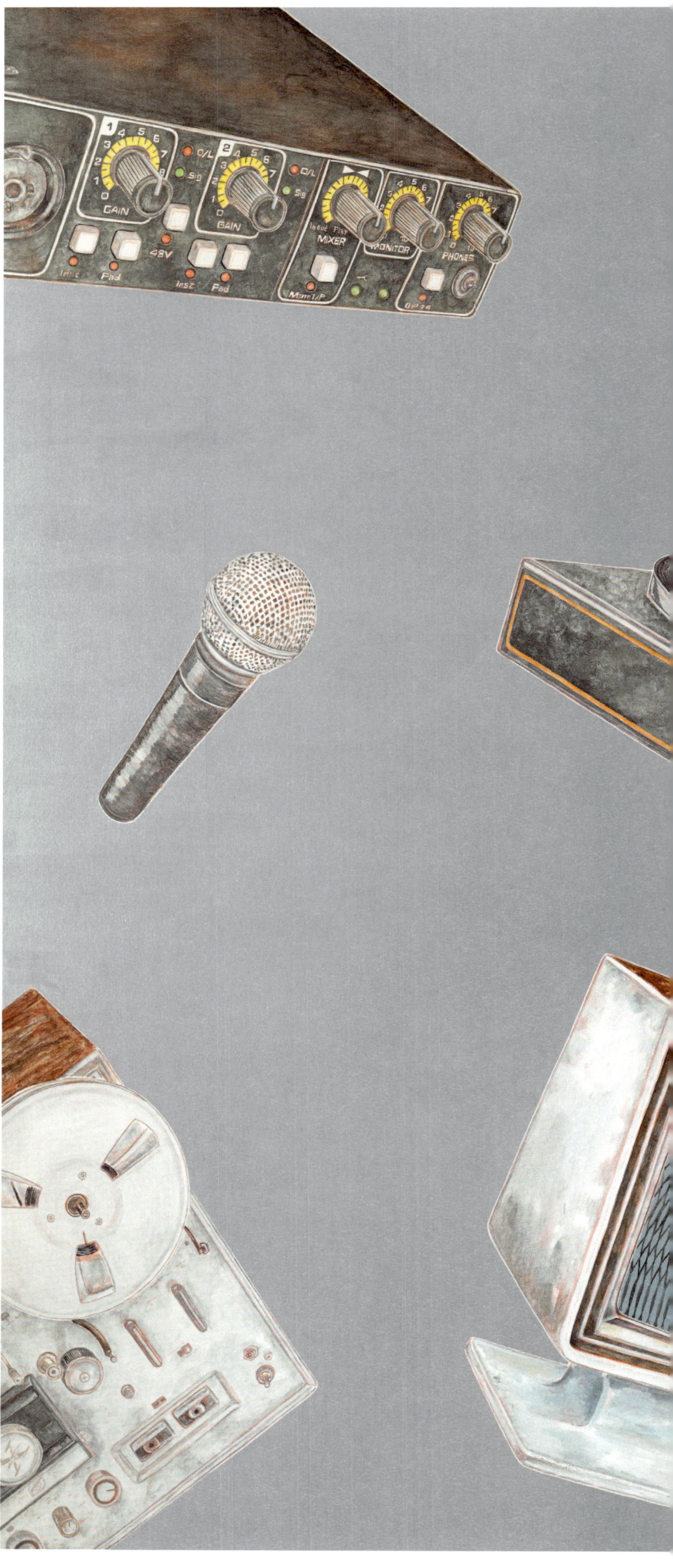
GAIN
C/L
Sig
Pad
48V
GAIN
C/L
Sig
Pad
MIXER
MONITOR
PHONES

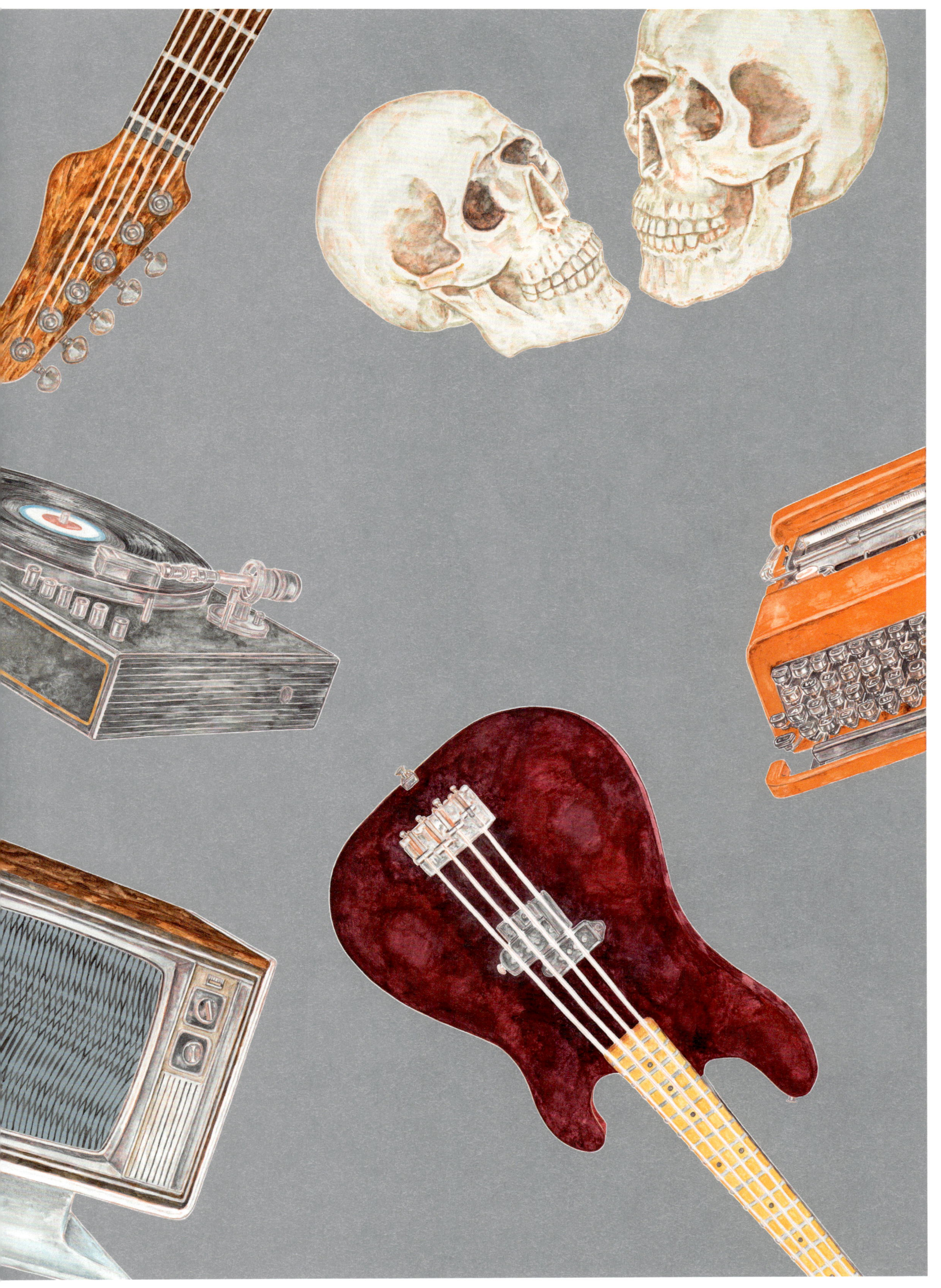

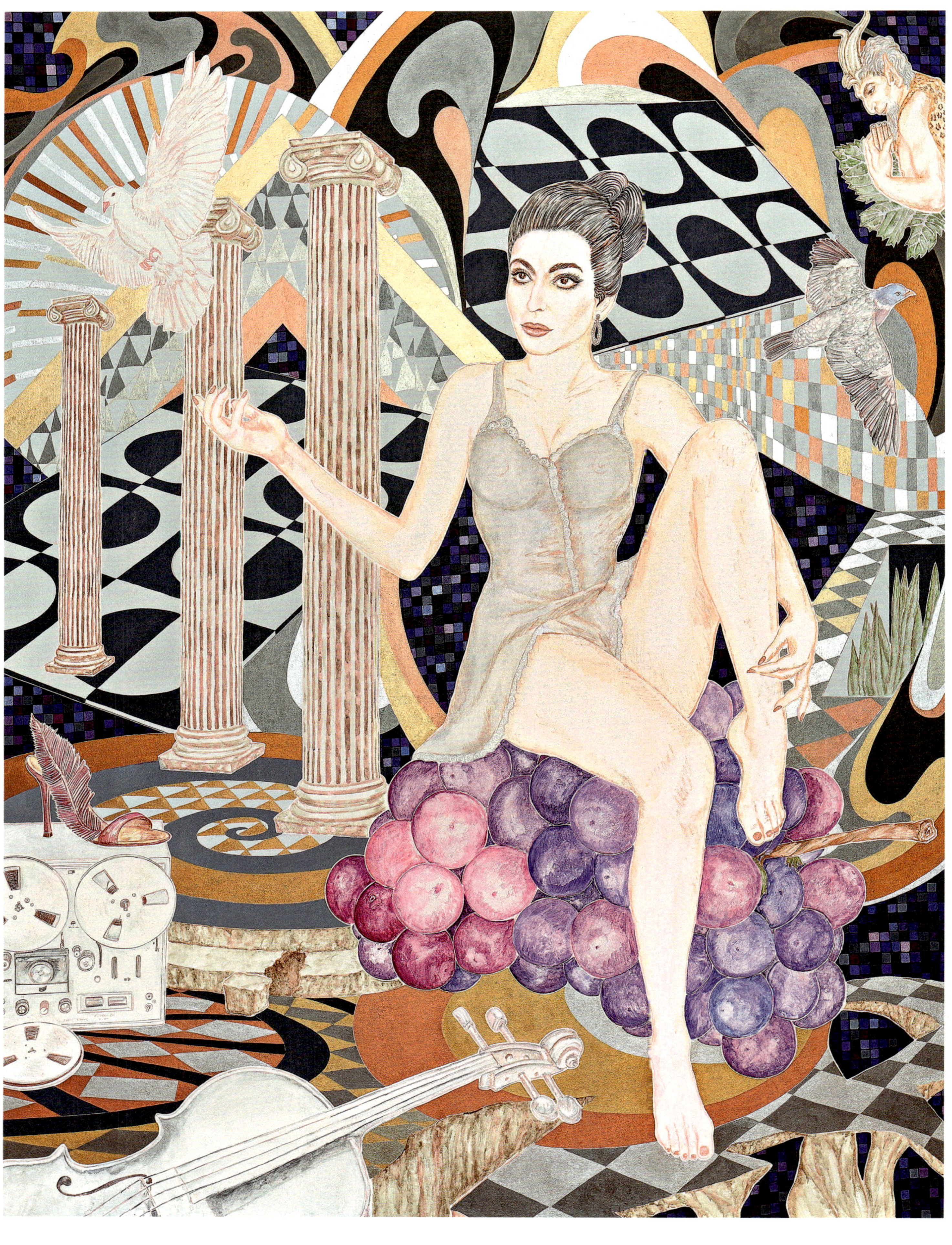

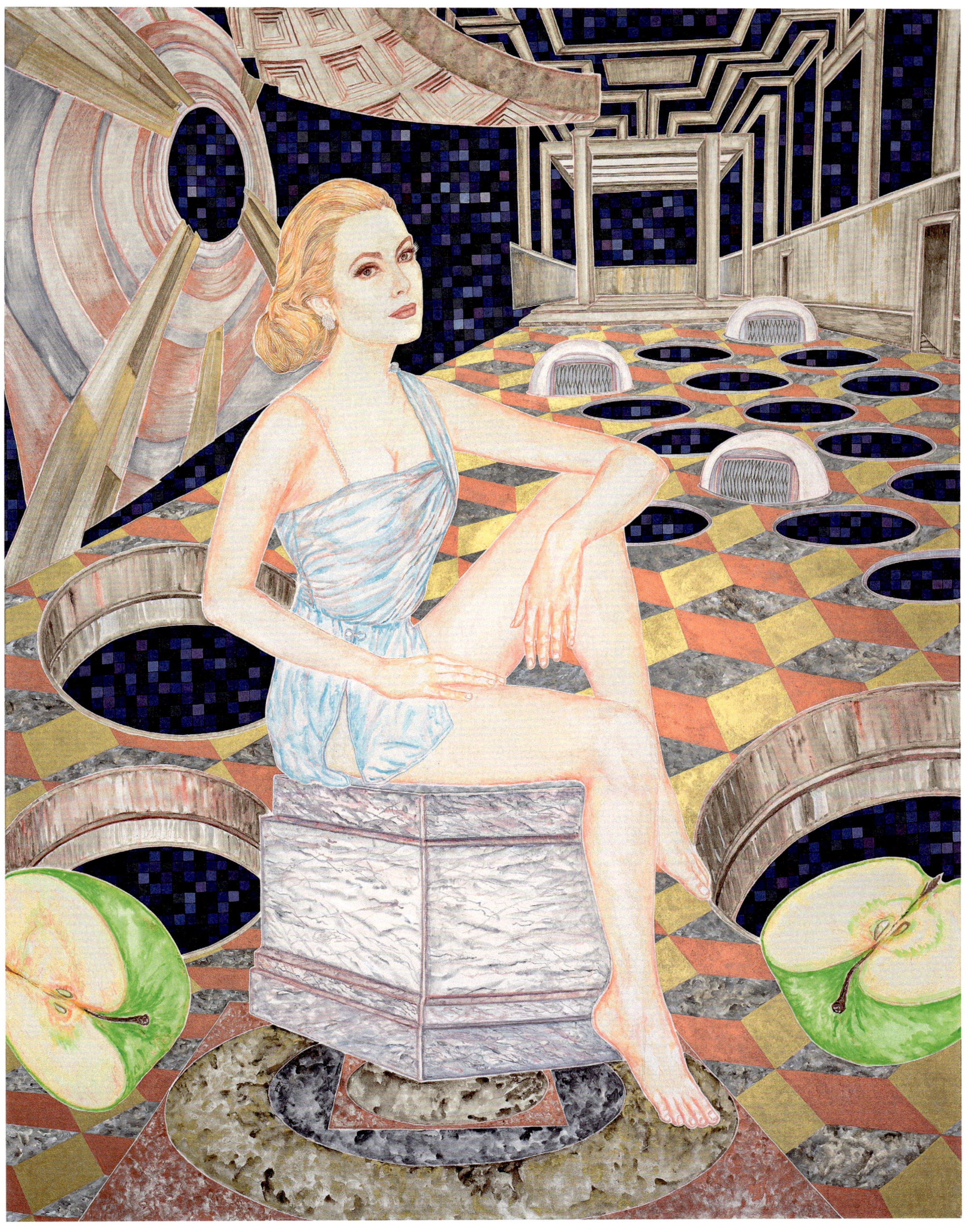

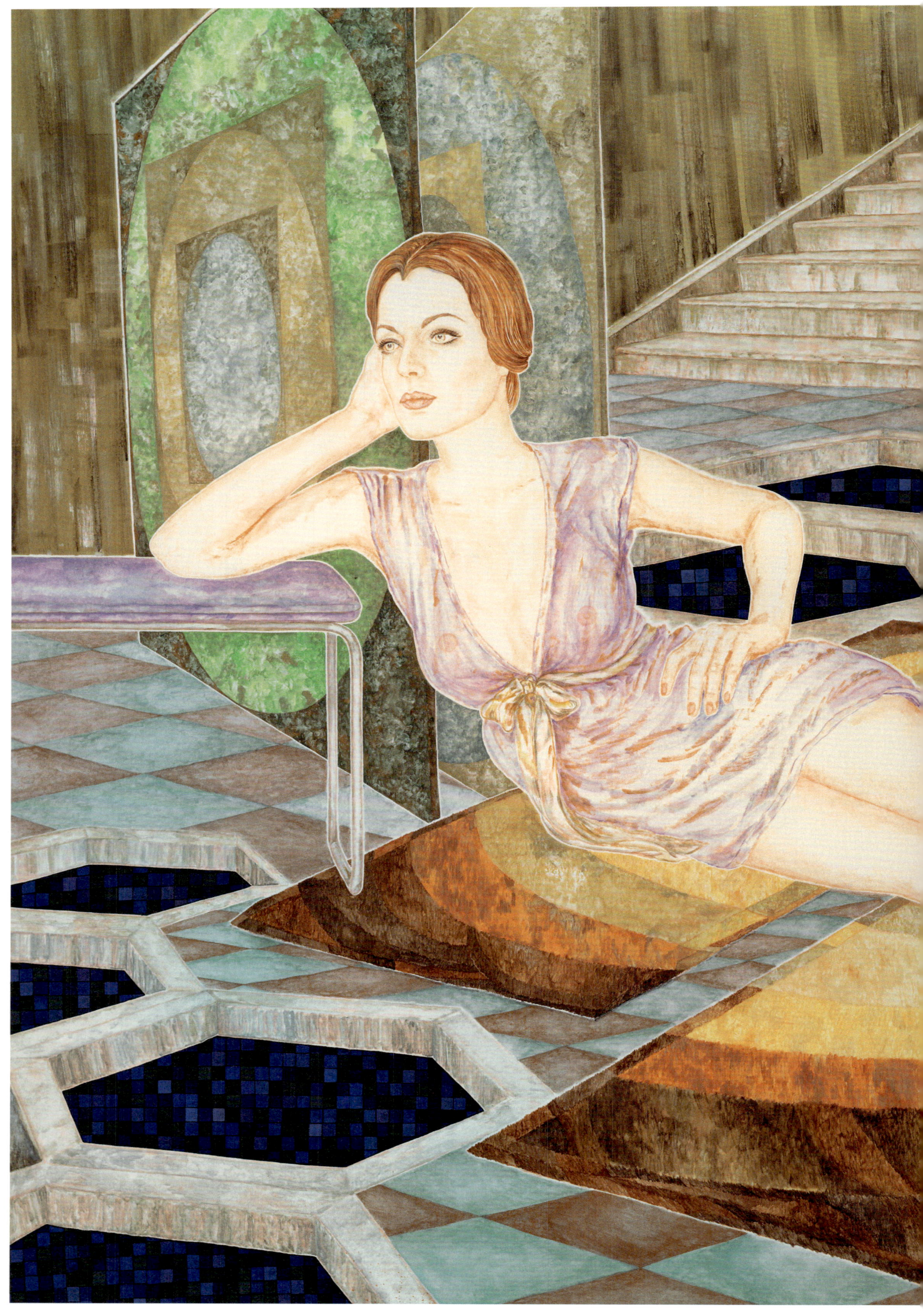

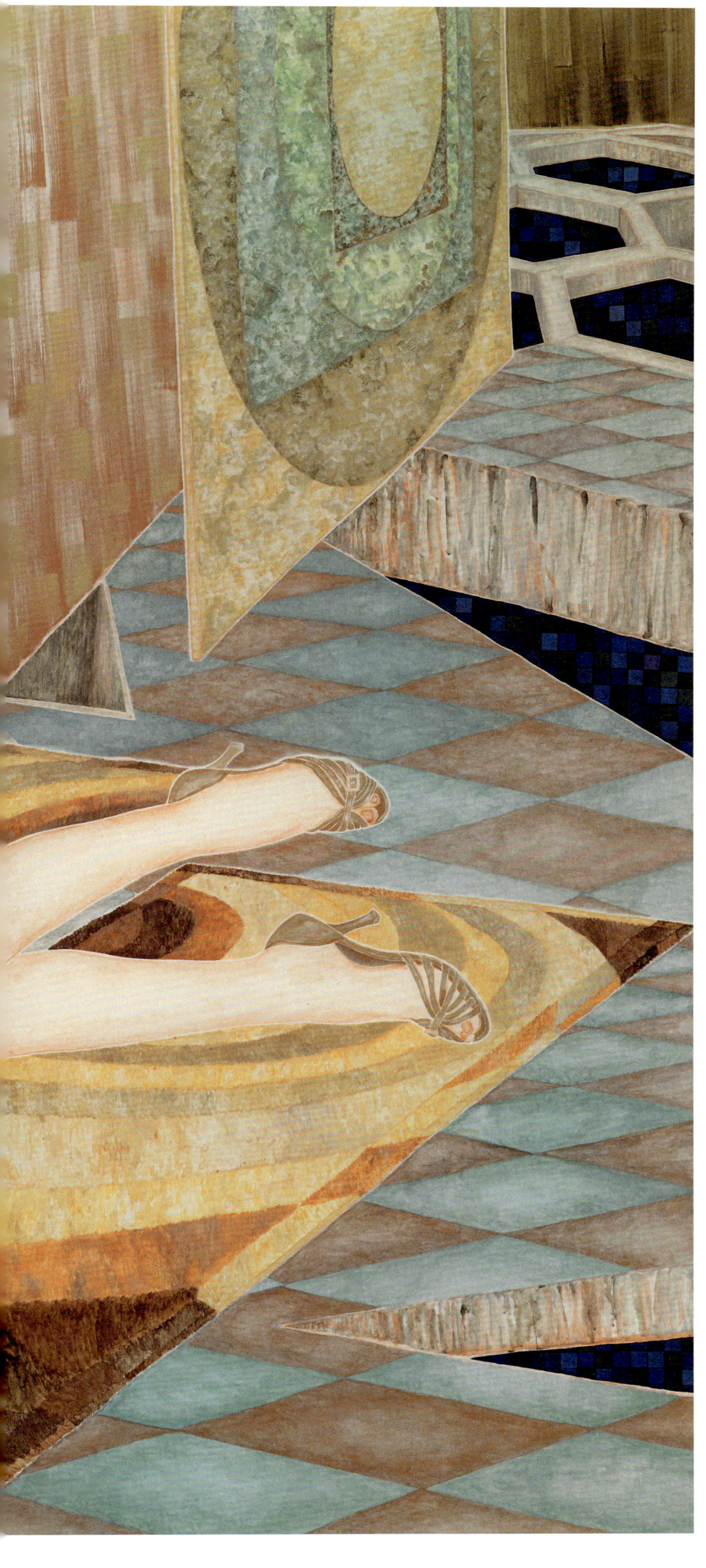

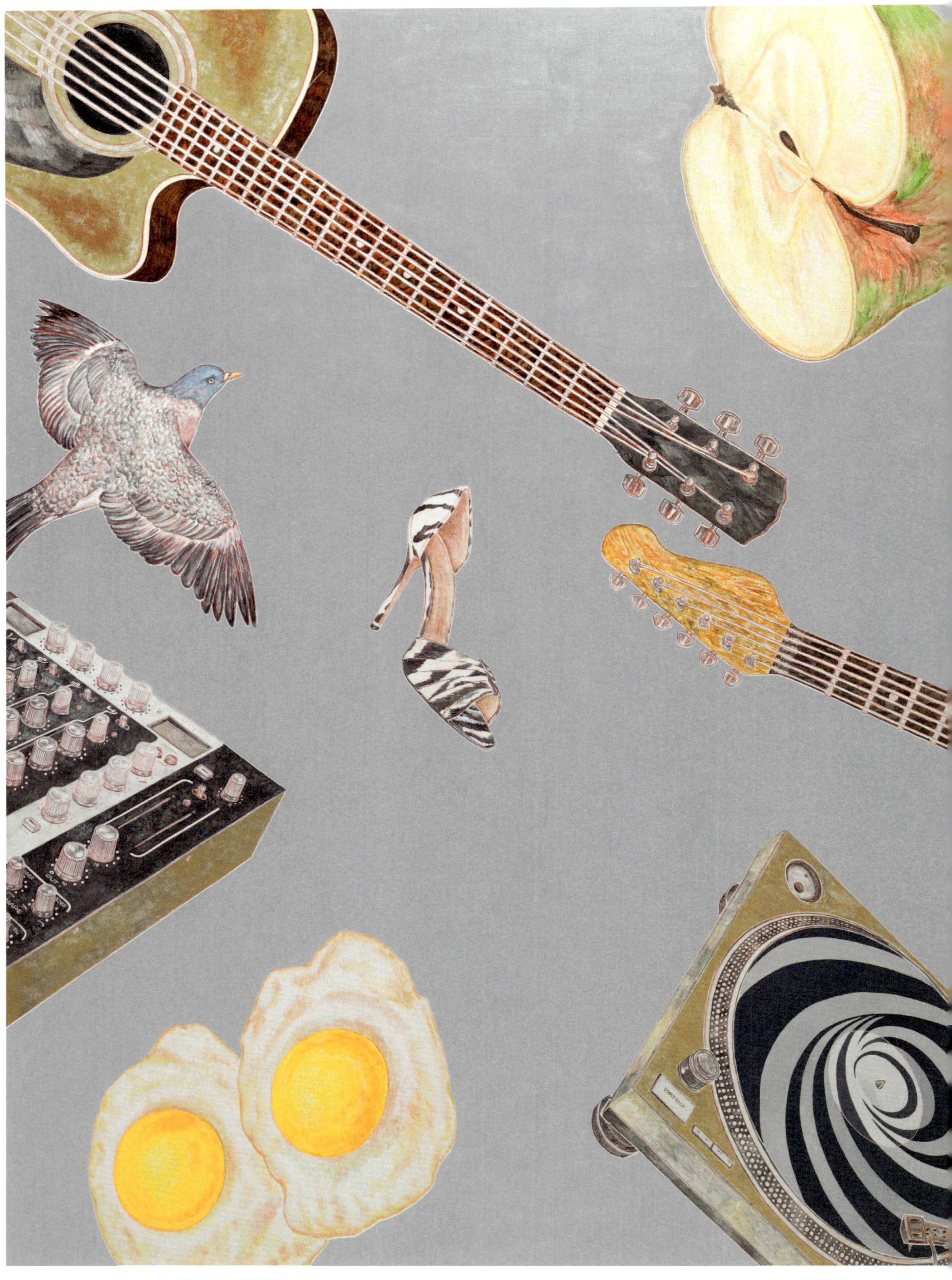

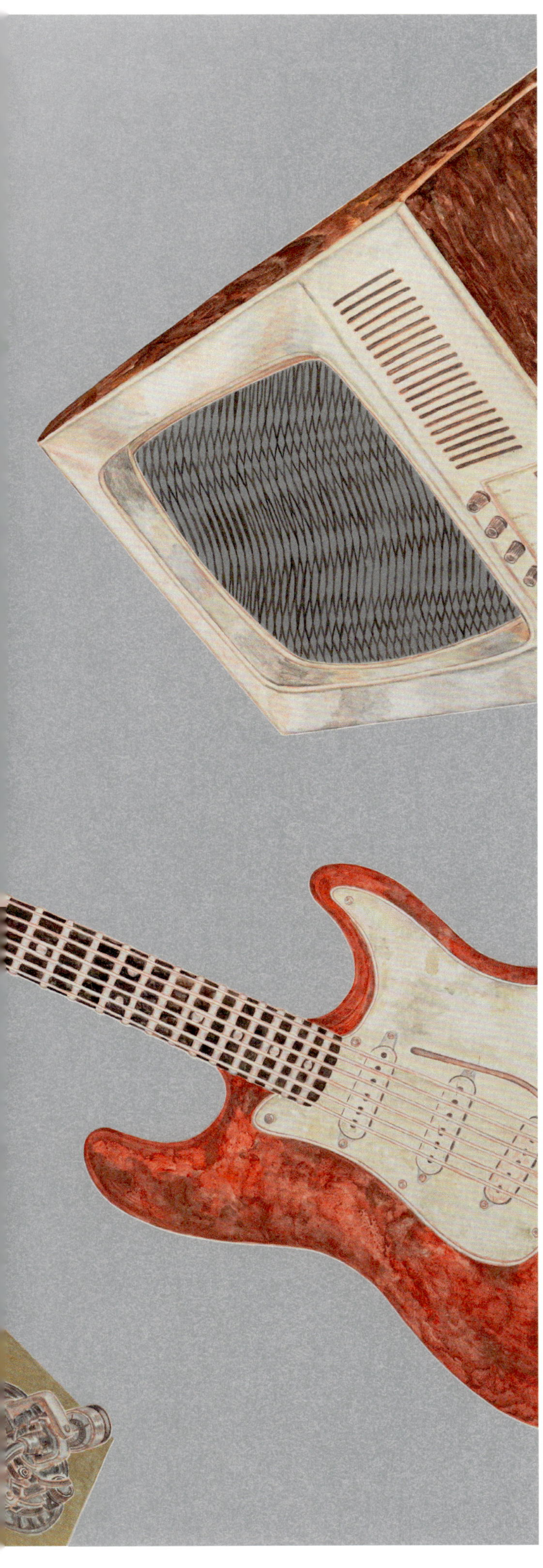

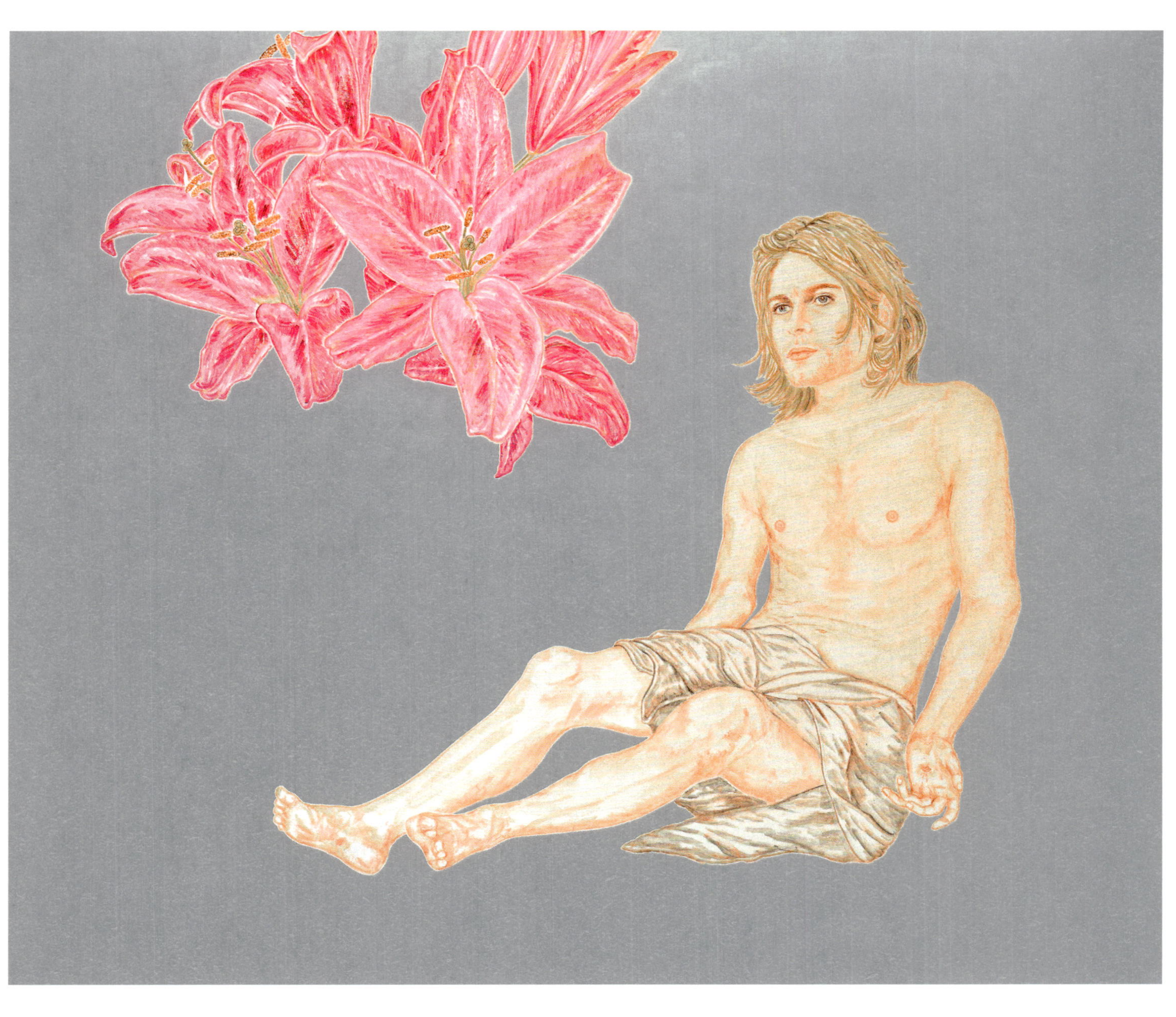

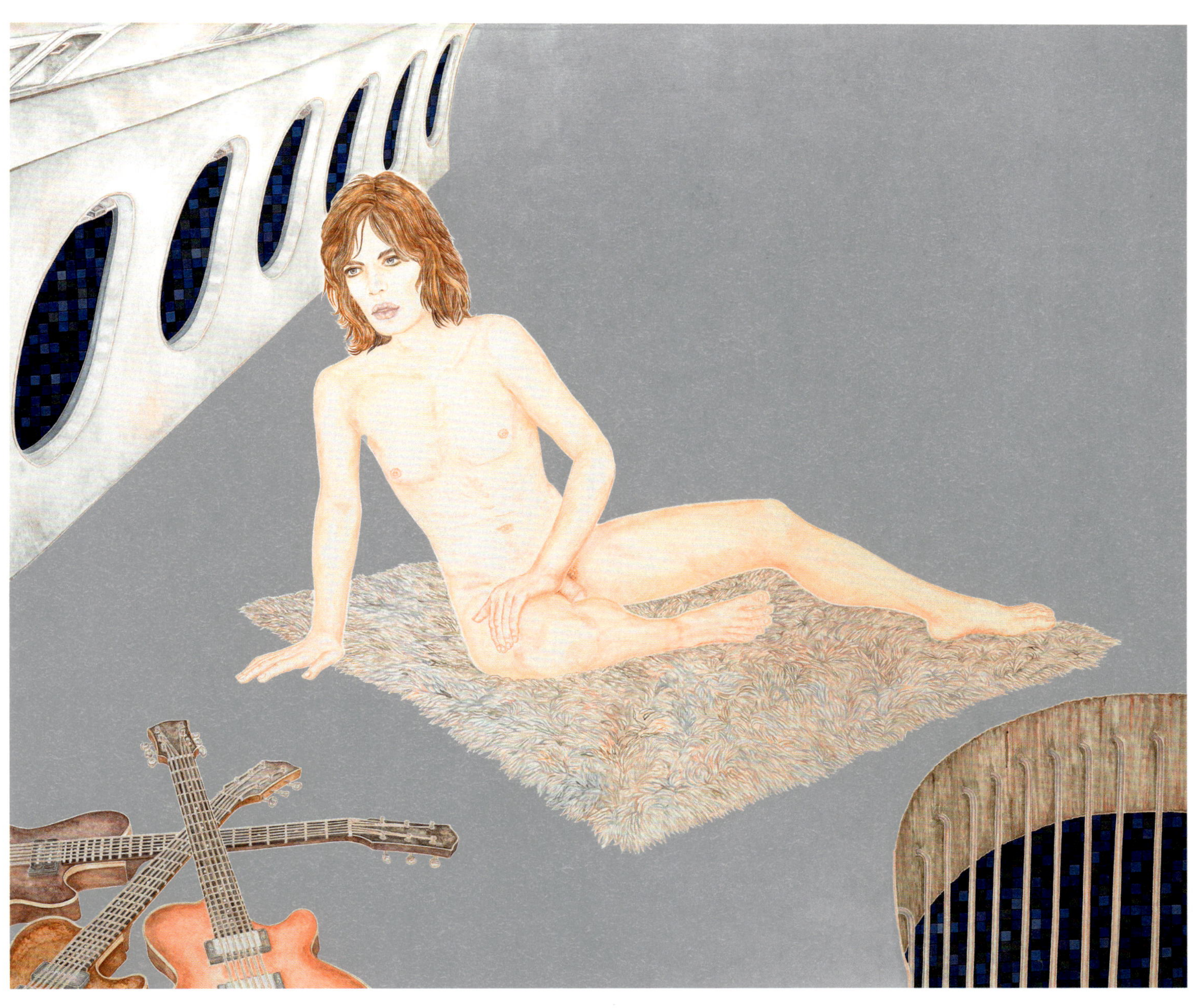

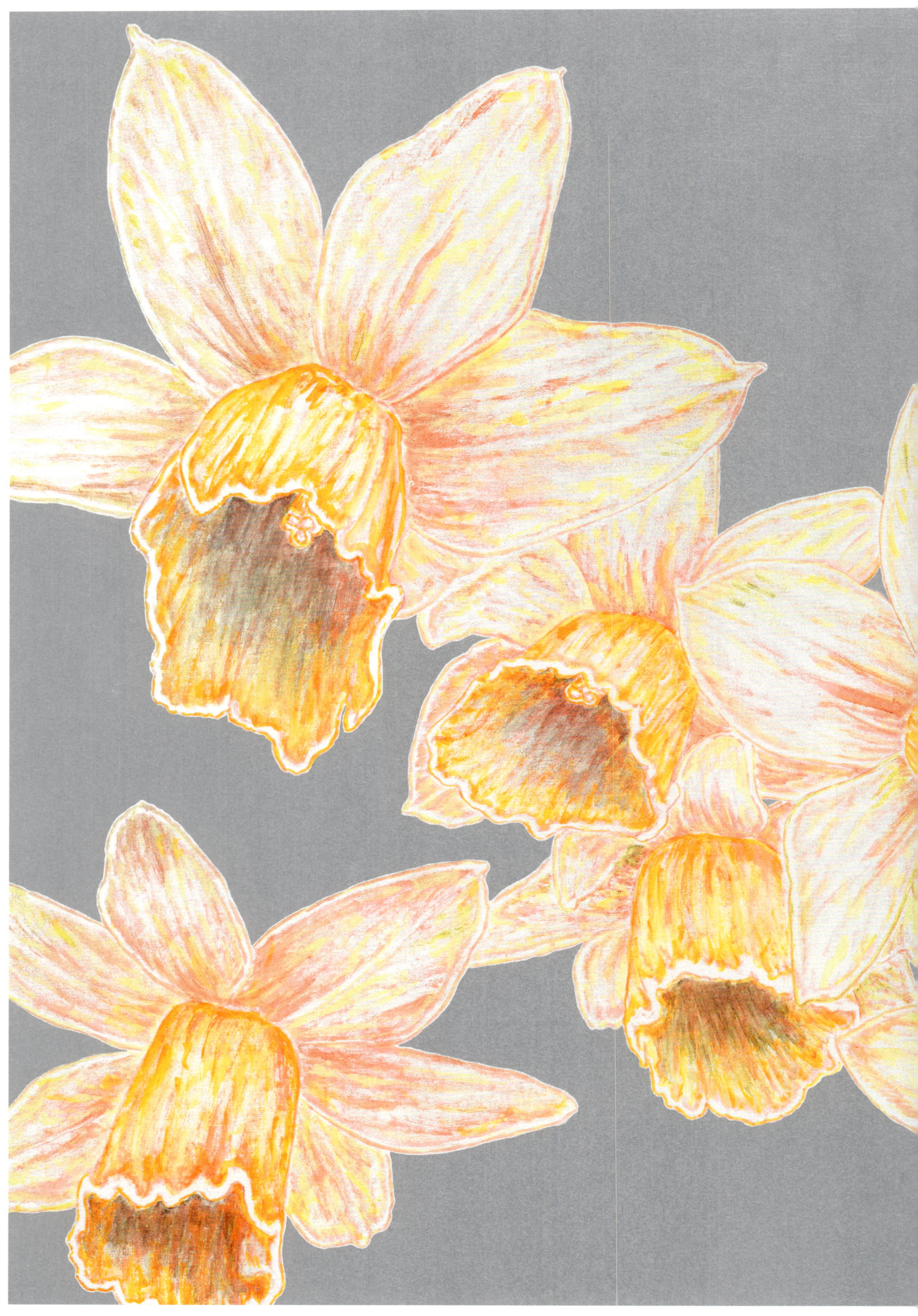

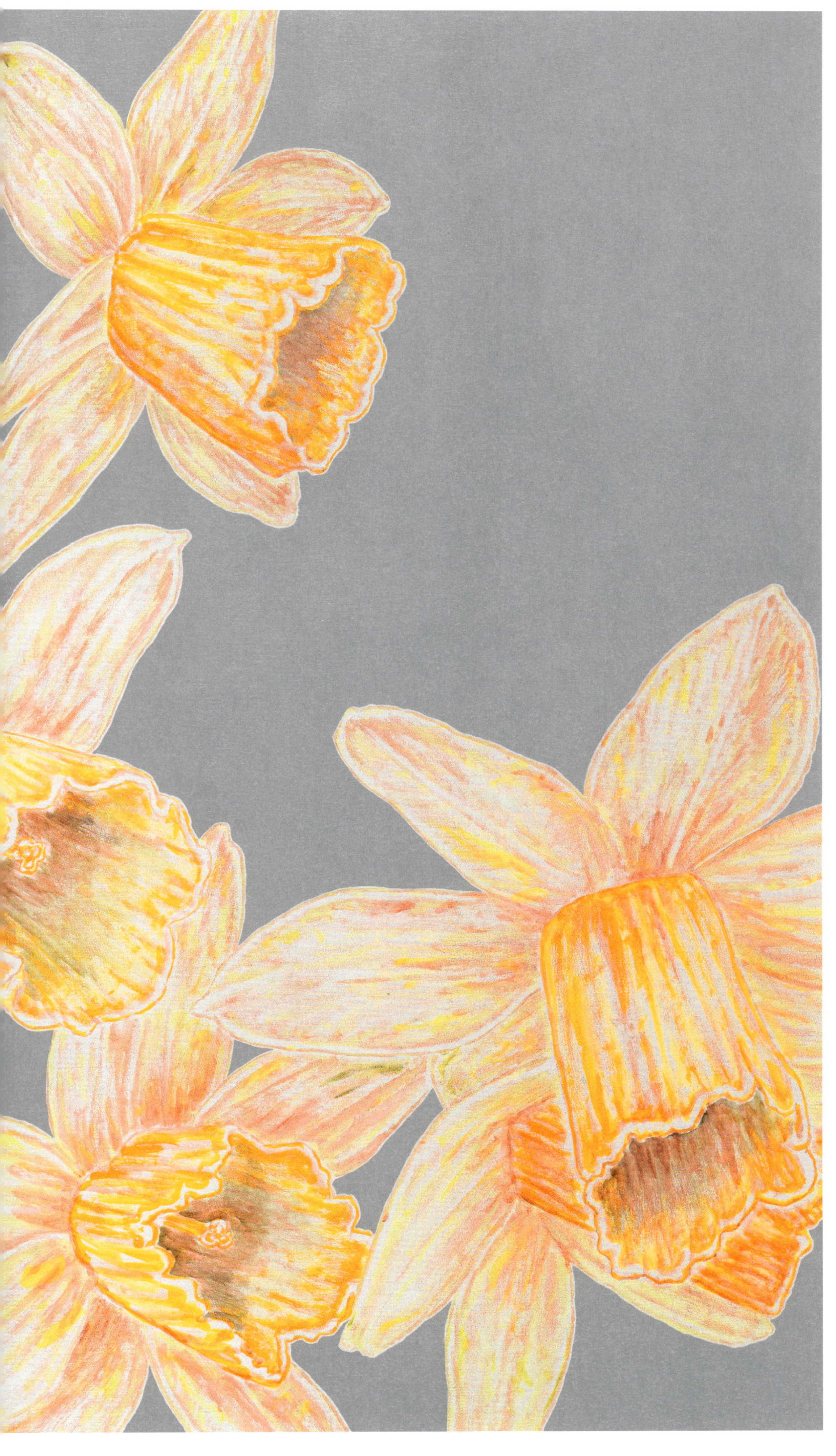

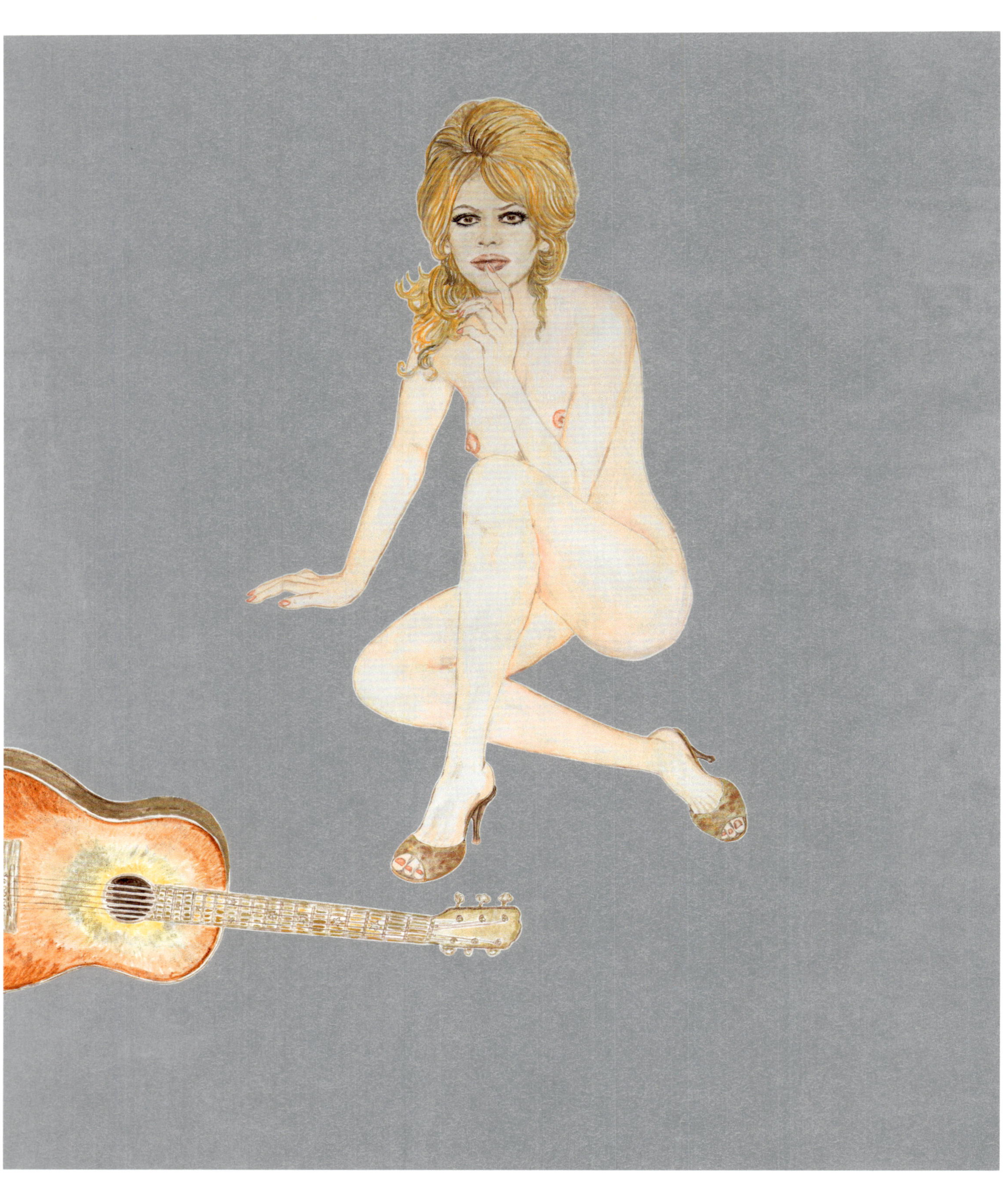

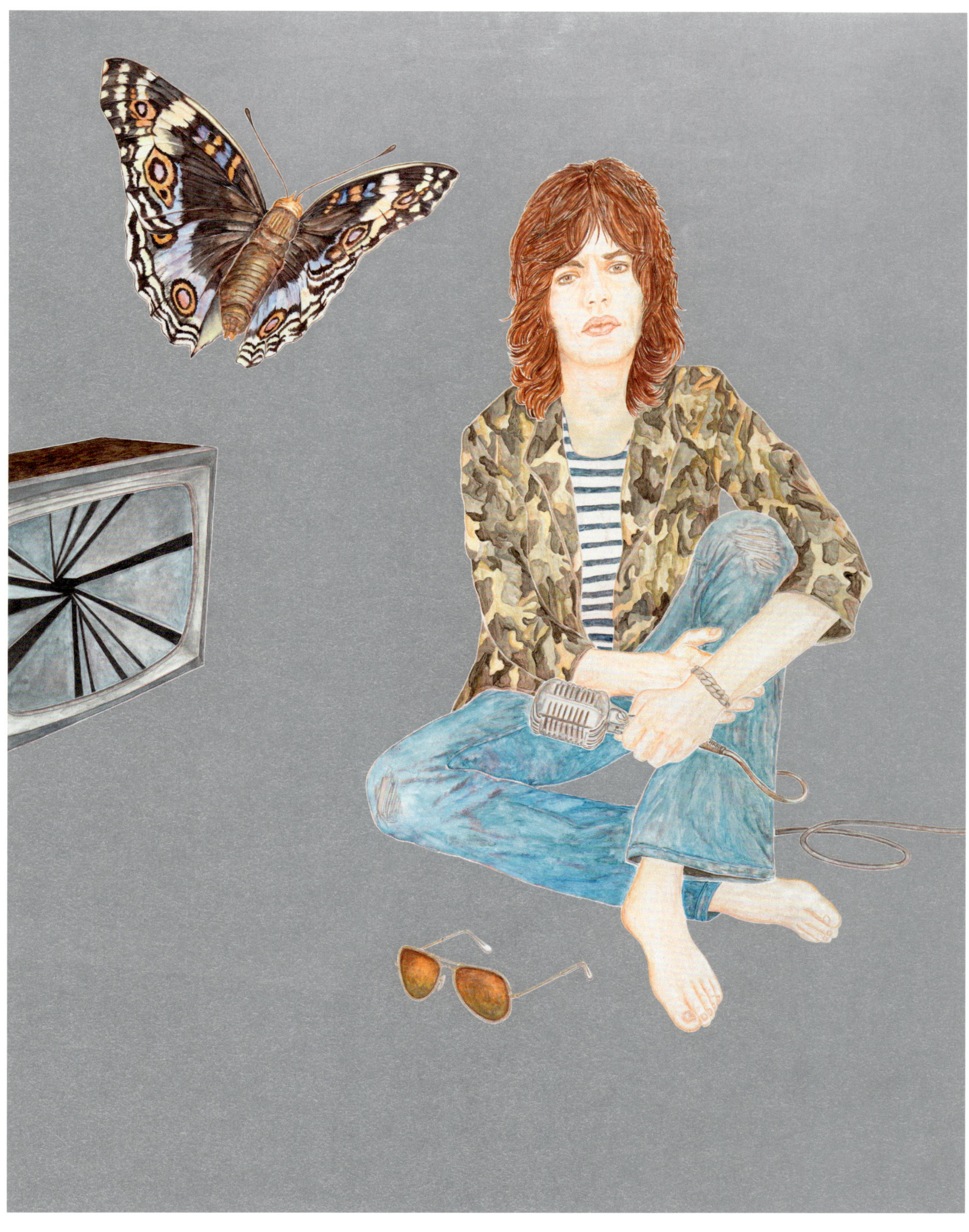

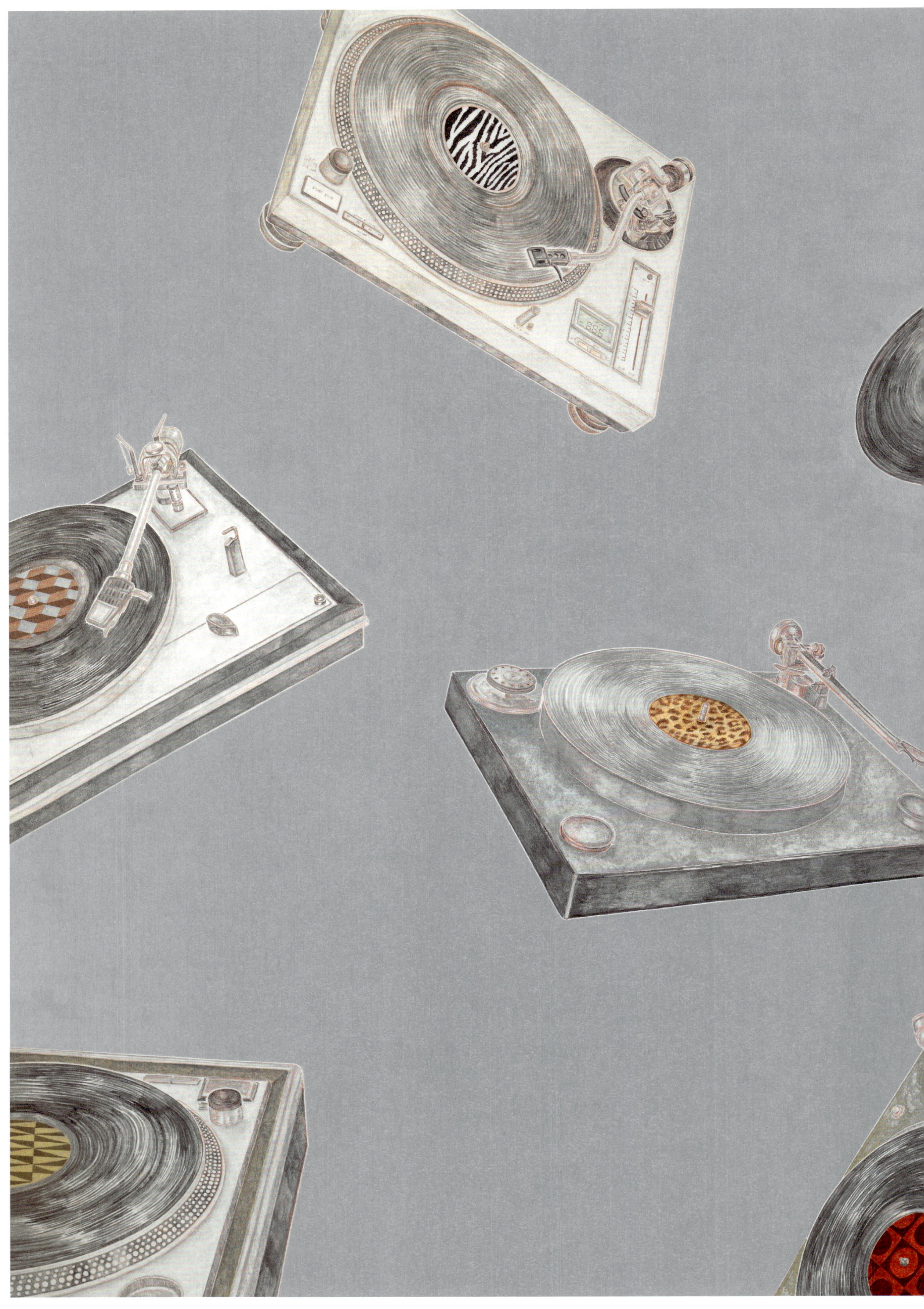

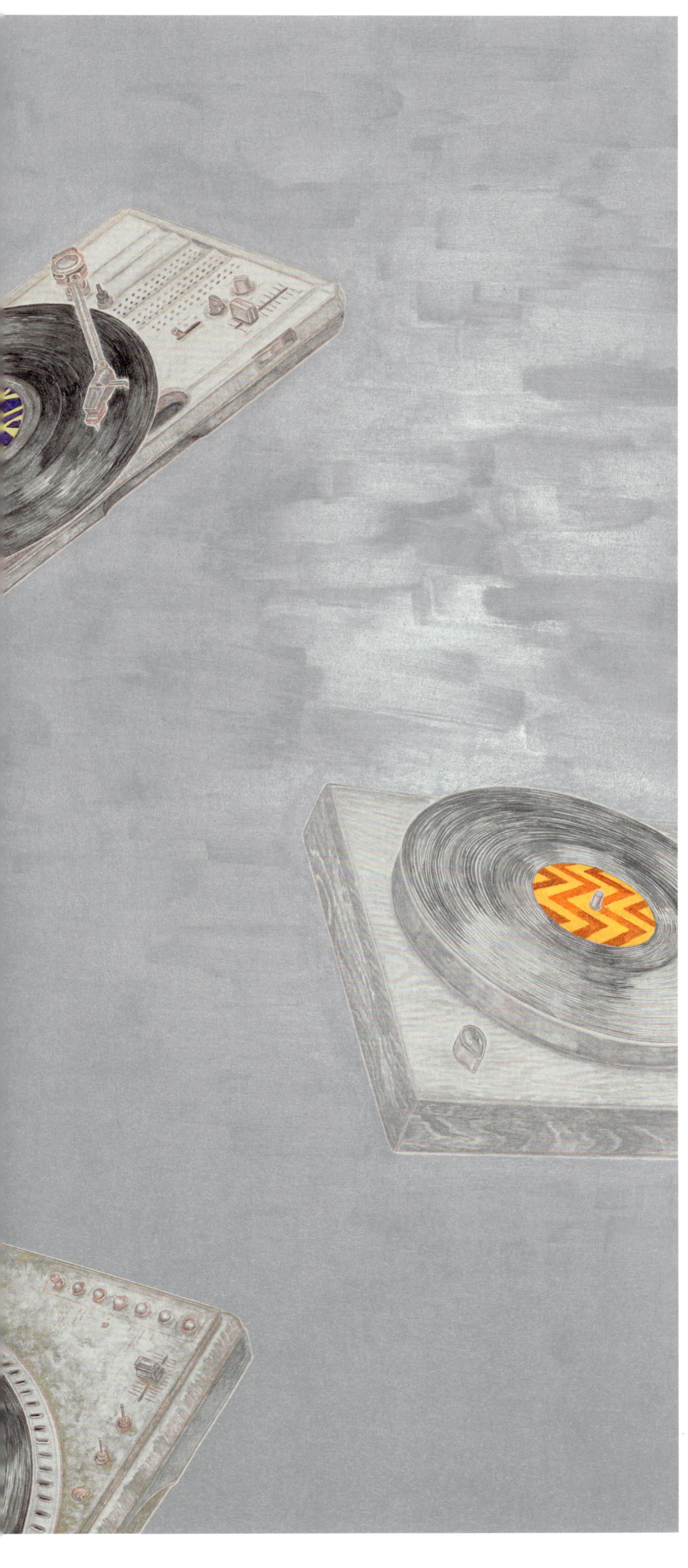

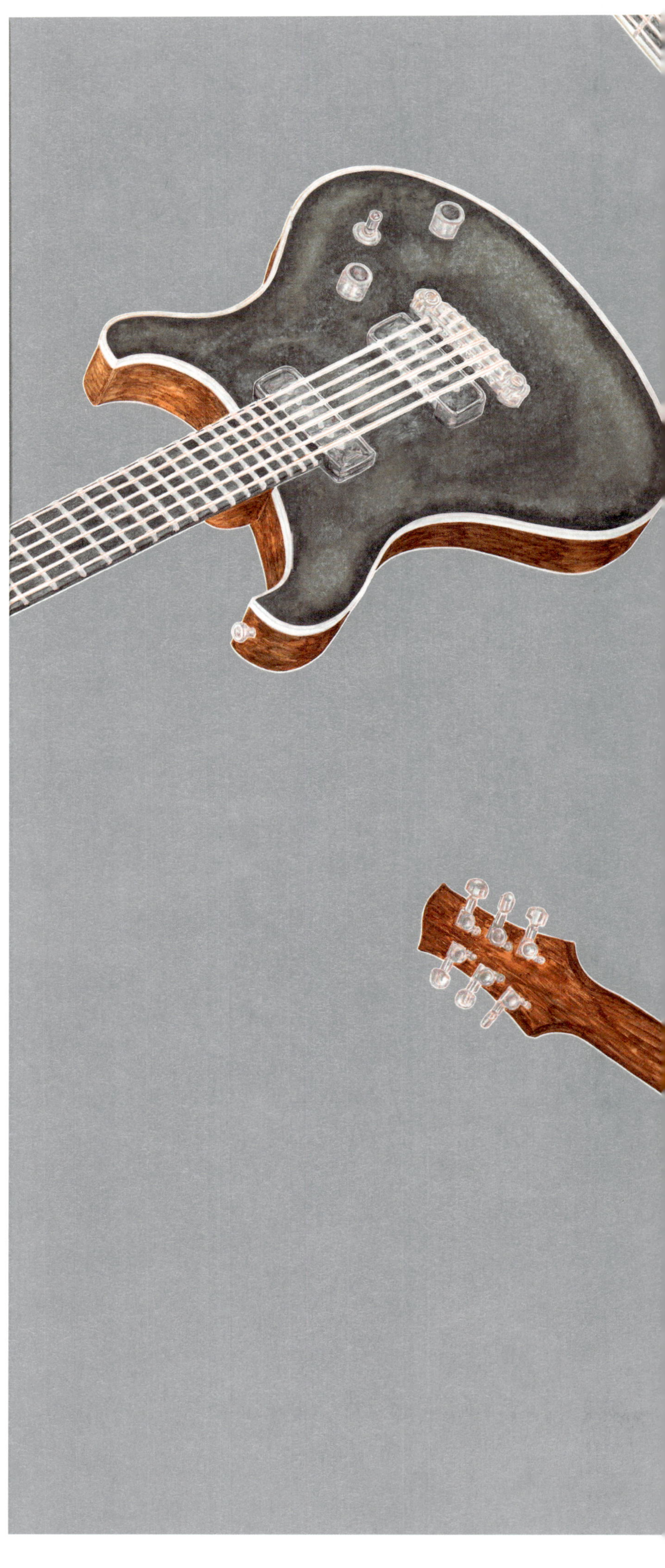